Maren Muter

A Simple Twist of Chocolate

Maren Muter

A SIMPLE TWIST OF
CHOCOLATE

MAREN MUTER

A Simple Twist of Chocolate

Maren Muter

The Chocolate Syndicate / A Simple Twist of Chocolate Copyright © 2025 by Maren Muter

All rights reserved. This book or any portion thereof may not be reproduced or used in any manner whatsoever without the express written permission of the publisher except for the use of brief quotations in a book review.

Publisher's note: This is a work based on non-fiction.

Printed in the United States of America

Edited, formatted, and interior design by Maren Muter

Cover art design by Maren Muter

p. cm.

Muter, Maren

A Simple Twist of Chocolate / Maren

ISBN-13: 978-1-7321128-9-6

First edition published 2025 10 9 8 7 6 5 4 3 2 1 0

A Simple Twist of Chocolate

Maren Muter

DEDICATIONS

To my Mary, Thank you for being my Mary. You were always in my heart - and always will be. Thank you for helping me write your story. It will continue into the next book - I'm glad you got to read it before you left. I love you. I miss you.

To my "Emily" Thank you for the ice cream cone cupcakes. And the notes on my desk, and for the jars to bury my letters. I love you, mom. I miss you.

To my David, There is not a moment you are not missed. And in every moment my heart holds you. I miss you dearly. I love you. I miss you, Davie, I miss you.

To my Gresham, Thank you for sharing this life with me. I am not sure how to express how much our time together means. But let me start with this. Number one: I love you... a tons!

To my Brandon, It seems as though we've lived a million lifetimes together all wrapped in one. From the chocolate explorations, to the unimaginable storm that crumbled the ground beneath us. I am thankful we get to share this life together. I love you. I love you.

A Simple Twist of Chocolate

Maren Muter

A Simple Twist of Chocolate

Chapter One	1
Chapter Two	9
Chapter Three	33
Chapter Four	49
Chapter Five	56
Chapter Six	70
Chapter Seven	91
Chapter Eight	110
Chapter Nine	132
Chapter Ten	149
Chapter Eleven	161
Chapter Twelve	168
Chapter Thirteen	189
Chapter Fourteen	196
Chapter Fifteen	218
Chapter Sixteen	227
Chapter Seventeen	239
Chapter Eighteen	261
Chapter Nineteen	273
Chapter Twenty	295

A Simple Twist of Chocolate

Maren Muter

Like a magnificent chocolate, this book
is 80% pure and 20% sweetener.

Some characters have been renamed for privacy.

A Simple Twist of Chocolate

Chapter One

Do not stand at my grave and weep; I am not there. I do not sleep. Several birds landed on the lawn across the tarmac as the unbidden words drifted in my mind. *I am a thousand winds that blow, the diamond glints on snow.* They bowed their heads, searching the wet ground for worms while the poem circled my thoughts. *I am the soft stars that shine at night.* They scattered, wings slicing the air, as they slipped into the distance. *Do not stand at my grave and cry. I am not there; I did not die.*

"Excuse me. I didn't hit you too hard, did I?" a young man asked while placing his bag overhead.

"No, it's okay, it's fine," I muttered, heart still tangled in the poem's echo. There is nothing quite like a near miss of an elbow to awaken you from a daze. At least he apologized, I thought.

"Good." He gestured, placing a hand on his chest in sincere

apology. I looked closer at his wreath-adorned collegiate T-shirt. "Veritas," he said, moving his fingers over the insignia while slipping into the plush leather seat by the porthole. "Means truth."

Having seen the wreath before, I asked, "Did you go to school there?" making a little small talk.

He nodded, "Harvard Law," and kept talking as he worked to settle in for a moment, adjusting things here and there like nesting in preparation for the long journey. Once settled in, he wiped a clammy hand on his jeans and attempted a more formal introduction. "I'm Damion."

"Nice to meet you, Damion," I said, rubbing my head before carefully stowing my own precious cargo.

"Sorry about that. I hope I didn't hurt you." He said, chiding his clumsiness.

"I'm only teasing. Your elbow hit the seat . . . just let me know when you get up to stretch so I can prepare."

"Sound good."

I pushed my arms forward. Lately, it seemed, my muscles and older bones reminded me of their tiredness, sighing after all the long days, the speeding years, the eras which had passed. My body just wanted to sleep, to fall inside the memories and touch those it longed for.

Passengers shuffled along like hourglass sand behind us. Pushing as a narrow procession onto the plane, irritated when forced to stop every three feet while bags were placed into the overhead compartments; a few thankfully left the mechanized march, finding places in our small business section of the plane.

"You on vacation?" Damion asked as he once again began rearranging his temporary home.

It is curious the reasoning behind a person's inherent need to segregate moments into categories, like perforating sections into a bar of chocolate. When all our moments move fluidly together. I shook my head. "I was away saying goodbye to someone in Varanasi. Well, an attempt to say goodbye."

"Oh . . . I'm . . . sorry . . ." Damion raised his eyebrows, playfully confused. "Sort of?"

"Don't be sorry. I think in the end, the very end, he was content. I hope so anyway."

"Glad to hear it." His attention shifted to the window while the faint red glow of the seatbelt signs momentarily held mine, along with the hum of quiet conversations built between passengers. The polite tidbits about themselves melding into the white noise of the plane. How varied their stories must be, how different each life is. No, let me take that back. When it boils down to it, our stories are similar, filled with various experiences;

the difference is how we see them, feel them, and weave within them.

The captain's narrating voice entered the cabin. "Flight crew, prepare for departure," his British accent scratched above the plane's hum. "Flight 817 should arrive in New York in a mere sixteen hours and fifty-five minutes. Enjoy the ride."

The plane pushed back from the terminal, its heavy tires pressing into the cement. The previous week felt like a dream with flashing images of Mumbai and Varanasi. And in the blur of ascent, another image surfaced, snowflakes drifting serenely beneath a lamppost, dark skies hiding the world away, leaving only the weight of his body in my lap.

Racing down the runway, the Boeing 787 climbed steeply until leveling off, the roar of the jets lost in the clouds. All was hushed, peaceful. The zipper on Damion's black bag slid along smoothly. He picked out a book, The Adventures of Huckleberry Finn.

"One of my favorites." I said.

He glanced at the cover, "A little adventure for the flight."

"Well, between Tom Sawyer and Huck Finn, I am sure you'll find it. What was in India for you? Did you explore the sights?" I asked.

"Nope, a meeting." His hand ran over the worn cover of the

closed book. "How 'bout you? Where do you head after New York? Did your friend live in Varanasi? Was he Hindu? Stupid questions."

"No. Not stupid. He wasn't Hindu; he was Jewish but not religious. He traveled quite a bit. When he was in India, years ago, he'd become quite intrigued by the region's history and traditions. One being the scattering of ashes over the Ganges River in Varanasi. So, he and his friend started a service transporting ashes from the US to Varanasi for a recorded ceremony scattering them on the river, when their families couldn't do it. And that's where I took him. I am a louse, though, because, he is still in my bag... You see, his whole life revolved around money, but the fates had other plans. They chipped away at his fortune, through his greed. They sent thieves and conmen, storms and weather, and quickly aged houses, all to say, 'You can't take it with you.'"

"You have him with you? Didn't he want his ashes scattered? And greed? Doesn't that contradict the service he created?"

"Yes, he's with me." I looked at my carry-on. "And no, he did not ask for his ashes to be scattered there. I just thought it would be something special. He always said no one did anything nice for him, but at the last minute, right near the bank of the river . . . That's when I changed my mind. As for the service he started, it was such an interesting idea. It's not that it wasn't meaningful—it's just that, knowing him... it was more of a good story to tell than compassion." My eyes scanned an invisible film, playing 8mm scenes of the man. "Or maybe it was, maybe it was his way of feeling connected to the idea of family."

"So, was that nice or not nice? Not spreading his ashes." Damion asked while catching the eye of a young flight attendant with "Madge" etched into her silver wing tag. She interrupted our revelatory exchange by offering drinks. "I'll have a sparkling water, please," Damion said. "With lime." He reached for the drink, taking a small sip before placing it on the tray table.

"I guess a better question is," he restated, "what are you going to do with him now?"

"Well. For now, I'm heading back to New England — Vermont. And his ashes can join me there." I looked again at the worn book cover on Damion's lap. "Would you like to read?"

"In a bit. There's plenty of time." Opening his bag once again, a more sensual object was the focus of his attention. A small brown paper-wrapped box, stamped with a label and secured with twine. Carefully, he untied the tiny twine knot, removed the paper wrapping, and opened the box. The internal wrapping of parchment crinkled sharply as he spread it apart, which exposed several small dull pieces of chocolate. Lifting the contents closer, he breathed in the deep, amalgamated, earthy scents of the beans which had created them. One of the small, jagged chunks met his lips; and I doubted he knew the real journey his savory treat had taken before finding its way into his hands. "What's in Vermont?" he asked. "Is that where you're from originally?"

My mind raced through the maple trees, climbed over the snowbanks, and let the question float like a raven beneath the sun. "What's in Vermont?" I echoed, tilting my head. "Maple syrup. Ice cream. Four seasons."

He raised an eyebrow, waiting for more. When I didn't continue, he held out the small box, tilting it toward me. "Want to try some?"

I studied the dark, jagged pieces. "Maybe later." Then, I looked at him. "Seeing what is in that box, you might like to hear a story."

"What kind of story?"

"One that, if we're being technical, started thousands of years ago."

His voice cracked. "Thousands?"

"We won't start that long ago. We'll start somewhere more like," I said, shifting to ease the weight from my hip. "Once upon a time..."

He tucked Huck Finn into the seat pocket in front of him.

"There was a woman, Ariel, who was practically created into being through a simple twist of chocolate. She was a consultant for an investigative group and international research." I paused for a second as the story gathered round. "And that's where we will begin. But things change, when she meets a man named Greg."

The hum of the vent above clicked off. As if on cue, Madge, the flight attendant, passed by with a tray of coffee, pausing before us. She looked at Damion, who declined with a wave of his hand.

"How'd she meet him?" he asked, matching the lingering gaze of the flight attendant.

"It was Ariel's work partner Stuart who brought them together. Stuart tended to play on her shyness—well, her introspection—which was usually fun but could sometimes be slightly annoying, as in the case of Greg's introduction. But let's start with Ariel and go from there."

***

1988

A hundred seventy. The folded bills pinned guilt in her hand, payment for the things she sold from her parents' garage as she sat between the frames of a phone booth. She sat inside the phone booth, its safety glass a thin wall between her and the world.

"I can't go back," she said into the narrow space, crouched on the floor, where the sun finally gave way to darkness, and the flickering neon lights above the store hummed. For two weeks, this phone booth was home until the last of her dollars stretched for a taxi, where an interview awaited.

With a deep breath, she straightened her shoulders, and she knocked on the brass plate.

"Just a minute!" called a muffled voice.

The lock rattled, releasing its hold on the weighty door. Ariel quickly combed fingers through her long disheveled hair.

"Ariel?" asked the middle-aged woman on the other side of the door.

Ariel nodded, gripping tightly to the hem of her cardigan.

"I'm Amanda."

Chapter Two

"It's good to meet you," Amanda said, stepping aside, letting Ariel walk through. "Come in. My husband Peter is in the kitchen and will be joining us." Ariel noticed that the gentleness of Amanda's mannerisms brightened her otherwise monochrome appearance.

Like Amanda, her husband, Peter, did not carry many memorable physical traits. He had an average build, 5'10", sandy blond hair that was partially balding, blue eyes, and nice teeth. He was muscular but not built as if he had gone to the gym. He was thoughtful, and his investigative mind was ever engaged.

Ariel stirred her tea—clockwise, *one, two, three,* she counted the gentle rotations before setting the spoon precisely across the saucer. Her posture, poised.

The initial interview was meant to last for fifteen minutes— just a quick meeting about helping with the children. But over an hour had passed, and she was still there, asking thoughtful questions about the kids' schooling and the books lining Peter's office shelves.

"She's not what we expected," Amanda said once Ariel had stepped into the kitchen to rinse her cup.

"No," Peter replied. "She's more."

There was one catch: she was underage.

"We will need to get your parents' permission before you can start with us." Peter looked directly into her eyes, "will this be problem?"

Ariel thought for a moment, her mother weeping, her father stoic, and shame flooded her chest. *I'm sorry, I'm so sorry.* "It won't be a problem. It will be ok," she said reassuring herself more than Peter. Ariel wrote their home phone number on a piece of paper and gave it to Amanda.

As many days over the last few months, sunlight puddled beneath the windows in the playroom. Ariel turned the final page of Sylvester and the Magic Pebble.

"And so," she said softly, "Sylvester came back, and the pebble stayed on the mantel, just in case."

The little girl in her lap gave a happy sigh. The boy, older by three years, rolled onto his back dramatically. "I wish I had a magic pebble."

"You do," Ariel said, brushing his curls from his forehead.

"I do?"

She tapped his chest right when a knock sounded on the doorframe. "Right there. Better than a pebble.your hear. That's really powerful magic."

"Ariel," Peter interrupted, eyes smiling at the children. "When you drop them at preschool, I've got a quick errand for you."

She nodded, already gathering the book from her lap.

"There's a packet on my desk — file folder, says 'Trieste' on the tab. Just hand it off to Ted. He'll be at the cafe, corner of 3rd and Hanley. Nothing complicated."

"Alright," she said, rising. "Do you want me to say anything?"

"Just give it to him directly. Thanks."

He turned without another word, and the little followed his dad down the hall.

She lingered a moment longer, watching the dust glitter in the beam of late morning sun. *It is like snow without the cold,* she thought.

The next afternoon, Ariel stood at the kitchen counter, slicing apples for the children's lunchboxes. The repetitive thud of the knife giving her mind space to replay a moment at the café. A woman's glance, practiced softness, had felt uneasy.

Peter woke her from her thoughts as he poured a coffee from the carafe.

"Peter," she said, "At the café today... some woman was watching me hand Ted the packet. Not that people don't normally people watch, but this felt different."

"Watching Ted?"

"Not really. More like... the folder. Not enough to be weird, but..." She shrugged, placing the slices onto a plastic plate. "There was just. I don't know, she felt off."

"What'd she look like?"

Ariel thought. "Maybe early-thirties? Dark hair. 5'6" Maybe... it was hard to tell. Grey scarf, dark blazer. Kind of... elegant, in a professional way. Maybe she was a research scientist? Or a doctor? I don't think a lawyer."

He nodded. "That is a lot of maybe's. What do you have that isn't a maybe? What color was her hair? What makes you think her perfession was part of your maybe list?"

Ariel closed her eyes, scanning the woman from memory. "She wore a badge, it was peaking out from under her coat. Scripps Ranch. Her name started with a V."

Peter's lips pursed in thought.

"She say anything?"

"Nope. Just looked. I only noticed because… well, it wasn't the kind of look you get when someone's admiring your shoes."

Peter gave a short nod. "Those are good things to pay attention to."

The next morning, there was a new file on the hallway table — this one was marked with a different name. No more dropoffs. This time, she'd be researching. And so it was, Ariel moved from nanny to, errand runner, to working for Peter.

The air in Peter's office was always too cold, and it was quiet—dim light, no footsteps, just the soft hum of the IMB PS/2 computer.

Ariel sat alone, reviewing correspondence pulled from a secure envelope Peter had left on her chair. The words were vague, precisely evasive. She flipped a page.

"The roots have exposed themselves."

She paused. Not because it confused her—but because it didn't.

The phrase tugged at her like a child on apron strings.

She had been seven, kneeling at the base of the tree behind her childhood home. A letter in her hands. Folded once, then again.

Dear Flower Lady,

Why don't people say what they mean? Why does it seem like life is a play?

The letter was written with care and taken into the woods. Placing it in a glass jar, she tightened the lid and mailed it by gently tucking it back into the earth, beneath the root of an ancient pine.

That was how she used to ask her questions—quietly, privately, without expectation.

And now? She was no longer sending letters into the ground.

She was decoding them from the world around her.

The cryptic memo was slid into a folder and pushed into the drawer. Her fingers moved over the next report which looked like dry economic data. Shipping records, commodity trades, financial audits from corporations.

She wasn't sure when it had started feeling different.

At first, her work had been simple. Organizing files. Entering figures. Occasionally summarizes reports on market trends. Peter always said data told a story, and it was their job to listen.

But patterns started emerging.

A Swiss bank account linked to an offshore entity, its balance shifting by millions overnight.

A government official who had denied wrongdoing two weeks ago—now stepping down "for personal reasons."

And always, Peter watched the puzzle unfold with that sharp, dissecting look.

"Follow the anomaly." What should be there, that isn't. What shouldn't be there, that is.

She had written those words down months ago, when Peter first told her. It had seemed like a simple rule at the time. But now, sitting at her desk, Ariel wasn't sure if she was following the anomalies anymore—or if they were following her.

The office was quiet.

Peter had left hours ago, but Ariel stayed, something gnawing at the edges of her mind.

The files were all there—stacked neatly in front of her. The same numbers, the same trends she had been analyzing for months.

But it wasn't right.

She flipped back through her notebook, the pages filled with scrawled figures and shorthand notes she had taken in passing. Her eyes caught what she hadn't placed before.

A series of bank transactions, all tied to different companies— but all routed through the same three financial institutions.

She turned another page. A confidential memo she had transcribed for Peter. She hadn't understood the full meaning at the time, but now...

"Financial irregularities."

Her fingertips tapped the top of her thumb in slow succession.

This wasn't about catching bad investors. It wasn't just about money moving in the shadows.

This was organized, calculated, systemic corruption.

The next morning, Ariel stood in Peter's office, gripping the reports in her hands.

"These numbers," she said, voice steady. "The shell companies, offshore accounts, the banks. The government. This isn't good."

Peter didn't look up immediately. "Nope."

Ariel placed the folder on Peter's desk, flipping open the file. "The same shipments, the same routes, rerouted at the last minute. The buyers? All different shell companies, but every single one leads back to the same offshore bank." She jabbed a finger at the pages. "And that bank has ties to—"

Peter leaned forward, resting his elbows on the desk. "To what?"

Ariel swallowed. "To political campaigns. To trafficking. I read over and over last night; it isn't just drugs or money laundering; there is a different product, and I am afraid to guess what it is. And it is linked to a network that keeps shifting just enough to stay ahead. And now, this one," she pointed to the manila folder, "it's linking back to commodity manipulation—oil, sugar, grain, cocoa. But, Peter. There is more. I haven't figured it out yet, but it's more."

Peter finally looked at her. His face unreadable.

"Tell me how you put this together?"

"Well," she began, watching as the coordinates, account numbers, and names stirred from the pages and began pacing the room, pausing at her words to brush against the potted fern in the corner. "I followed the anomaly," she said instead. The anomalies froze. Eyes of ink and cipher locking onto her, now caught in a spider's web.

"When we follow the anomalies, that is why we are so careful. Even when they seem small. It is why we remain quiet."

"I guess. But we aren't doing anything bad… We are just researching, right?"

"A little more than that, Ariel."

He picked up a different folder, thinner, its contents far more disturbing. He flipped it open and slid a grainy photograph across the desk.

A man slumped behind the wheel of a luxury car, blood pooled beneath the shattered windshield.

"This was," Peter said. "An independent investigator. He was tracking the same offshore account we have on our desk when his car 'accidentally' went off a mountain road."

A laden weight settled in her stomach.

Images flickered through her mind like film reels catching on jagged edges.

A car twisted against the guardrail, its tires screaming as it lost grip. Metal buckling. The violent snap of steel as it plummeted.

A cracked windshield, splintered like a spider's web, streaked red in the morning light.

A man—the investigator, whoever he was—alone in the wreckage, the weight of his final discovery buried beneath the twisted remains of his car.

Ariel swallowed hard, but the visions didn't stop.

Peter pushed another file toward her. Headlines. A journalist. Dead in a hotel room. A former CEO. Suicide—after an anonymous tip-off ruined his career.

Ariel looked up, her fingers cold. "We're not just tracking

the fraud then, are we?"

Peter held her gaze. "We're tracking the people who make the fraud disappear."

Silence thickened between them.

Then Peter did something he rarely did—he softened, just slightly.

"I brought you into this because you recognize — you listen — you see beyond the box," he said. "Because this? This is where things stop being just numbers."

"You are fooling him. You are fooling yourself. He's gonna find out how stupid you are." Ariel's mind spun beneath her sibling's voice, which she did her best to push them out with all the late nights, the reports, the patterns. And the assignments weren't just business intelligence — they were battles in a war she hadn't even realized she was fighting. Then it was her own speeding voice of doubt that silenced her siblings', *"you're gonna get him hurt, just like you hurt everyone."*

The photographs reeled from their place on the desk. A string constitution though is what stood within her. A resolute heart that wasn't afraid to do what she thought was right.

Considerations of the last twelve months of working for Peter clicked together like a dissection puzzle, where she went from being an assistant to what he would call more of a "fact finder."

She'd grown up in such a jockeying world. Her father had dabbled in the grey, moving the family within tides of trust. After running for Congress as a pro-gun control Republican in Oregon in the 1970s and losing because of it, he'd become more of a rogue. For the family, money was prevalent and thick for a time. It was a mania of highs until the lows showed up, and control was lost.

Ariel watched the world spin within her father's mind. She had memorized the eyes, the innumerable, minute variations, until she could foretell future actions. She found the voice also carried such clues, along with the tiniest twitches a poker player looks for. She learned everyone carried tells. They were like fingerprints—unique to the individual.

When running away from home, Ariel left high school early. She attended college for only a brief period with Peter and Amanda's support, but quickly realizing that even the advanced classes she audited didn't align with the intersection of quantum physics and consciousness she had spent her life exploring. Her intellectual pursuits were then self-directed, focused on experience and deep research. And for two years, Peter, good to his word, covered the cost of her books, research tools, and specialized consultations. He even introduced her to experts in fields ranging from physics to philosophy. On this evening, however, instead of her usual dive into conscious exploration, an old Humphrey Bogart movie brightened her small one-bedroom apartment.

"Popcorn and an ice-cold root beer. That's just what this evening needs," she said to herself, grabbing a thin knit sweater from the folded pile in her closet. One quick scan of the apartment as she checked her pockets for her keys and cash. Her shoes by the door. The stack of unread books on the coffee table. The file folder she had left on the kitchen counter earlier that morning.

Except—

A chill pushed its way to stand next to her.

That folder. Neatly stacked. Closed. Was now, slightly open. A single page slid out just enough for her to notice.

Her breath paused.

She listened.

The image of the man in the photos flashed in front of her.

Has someone been here?

A finger of fear brushed her spine as she cautiously entered the kitchen, scanning the room, this time with more consideration. Nothing else was touched. No drawers rifled through, no signs of a break-in.

"It's just your imagination." She reassured herself, checking the locks and windows for damage. The locks were intact. No signs of forced entry.

All was quiet on the walk to the convenience store. A moist scent of ozone rose from the pavement and shrubbery bordering the sidewalk, only to be interrupted by the exhaust from an occasional car, one of which pulled into the dark rear parking lot of the gas station. The aftermath of a rare Southern California rain slurped beneath its tires.

"Here." A young woman about Ariel's age, nineteen, handed the bathroom keys back to the clerk. He hung them carelessly on the wall behind him.

"Pack o' Reds?" the woman demanded more than asked.

He grabbed one from the hanging rack above the register.

Ariel was at the cooler picking out her drink. Maybe a ginger ale instead of root beer... No, root beer it is. She collected the small winning bottle.

The door chimed, signaling the other girl's departure as she approached the counter.

"This all?" the clerk asked, more out of habit than inquiry.

"Yes, that's all. Thanks," she said, stacking change on top of the dollar before sliding payment over the counter.

As Ariel left the store, a man in the rear parking lot approached the woman who had left only moments before. He scanned the girl's face. He was looking for someone, which hastened the girl's steps; he moved in her direction. She was clearly uncomfortable by how her body tensed; a hand from Ariel's heart, pushed from within. *Get away. Run!* Ariel's brain yelled at the girl. Her feet began sprinting toward the girl. *Run! Get away!* her thoughts yelled.

No one else was around, and running toward the girl went against everything she had been told growing up. "You need to get help if you see something dangerous. Because if you try to help, there would be two people hurt instead of one getting rescued." Her brain spoke mater-of-fact when situations arose. Stating obvious. But, Ariel chose to ignore the recitation of rules, there was any time. If the girl was taken, even if Ariel got the number plate, she would be in real danger.

The man's car was parked beside the woman's on the driver's side. He leaned against the door for a second just to be intimidating. The woman backed away, going to her passenger's side while he laughed mockingly, watching her scramble through the seats, start her engine, and quickly drive off. Ariel withdrew instantly, heading back into the store, but, like the ocean, she should not have turned her back to the man.

He grabbed her.

"I've been waiting for you," he said with his hand over her mouth.

Ariel's feet dragged against the gravel, her heels kicking up stones as she fought the man's relentless grip. Every muscle in her body strained against him, but his hand—like a vice—held her wrist in place. The car loomed ahead, its black body like an omen in the immediate shadow outside the harsh streetlight.

"No! Let me go!" Ariel shouted, her voice cracking as she twisted her body, using all the force she could muster.

He didn't answer. He simply reached for the car door with his free hand, and when the hinges creaked, something inside Ariel snapped. She turned sharply, using her momentum to claw at his face, her fingers digging into the soft flesh around his eyes. He growled—a deep, guttural sound—but her resistance only seemed to fuel his determination.

"Stupid girl," he muttered, catching her other arm and shaking her violently.

She kicked wildly, aiming for his shins, his knees—anything to slow him down—but he was a mountain. At well over six feet and two hundred pounds, he absorbed her attacks with infuriating ease. When he grabbed the back of her neck, Ariel panicked. Her hands darted down, clawing at his crotch, twisting and pulling through the denim with every ounce of strength she had.

But he didn't falter. Instead, he shoved her into the car with a force that knocked the air from her lungs. She landed hard on the seat, her shoulder pressing against the buckle. Before she could scramble away, his massive hand pressed her head down between the seats, pinning her against the rough fabric of the upholstery.

"Know where we're going, you little snoop?" he growled, his breath hot against the top of her head. His hand tightened, forcing her lower as he climbed into the driver's seat.

"Let me out, please, let me out!" Ariel sobbed, her voice raw with desperation. Her mind raced, calculating her options: jump out at a stoplight, reach for the door handle—anything but this.

The engine roared to life, and the car jerked forward. "Don't worry, darlin'. I ain't gonna kill ya." His voice carried an awful sneer. "Just play with ya for a bit."

"Please," Ariel whispered, her voice barely audible over the pounding in her chest. "Just let me out."

He chuckled, the sound cold and hollow. "Know why you're in my car?" he asked.

Ariel stayed silent, her lips trembling as she bit back a sob.

"'Cause it was you I was waitin' for," he continued, letting the words hang in the air like a trap. "Know why?"

"No." Spilled quietly from her lips.

"'Cause you've been running around playing games for your little boss, stirrin' up trouble. And I've got a message for you that you're gonna to take to 'im." His hand lightened slightly, but not enough to give her room to move. The car swerved sharply, throwing her against the center console.

"That's why I can't kill ya. You understand?" His words were slow, deliberate.

"I don't know what you're talking about," she managed, fighting to keep her voice steady. "Please, just let me out."

The car came to a sudden halt, throwing her forward. For a moment, there was only the sound of the engine idling and her labored breathing. Then, his hand released her, and he grabbed her chin, forcing her to look at him.

"You tell your boss man, next time, this will be one of his little girls. Stop blow whistles."

Ariel stared at him, her mind frozen, her body rigid. "I don't know what you're talking about," she repeated, her tone even now as she forced herself to remain calm. "Please. Let me out."

He studied her, his lips curling into a cruel smile. "You tell him. Can you do that?"

"Yes," she whispered, the word escaping her lips like a prayer.

He reached over her, unlocked the door. "All right then, get out."

Sitting up, she found they were in front of her apartment. She didn't hesitate. She pushed the door open, stumbling onto the pavement, legs shaking beneath her. She ran to her door. Trembling hands did not help in getting the key into the hole. Should I look back? She looked just in time to see the car pull away, her body too numb to move.

In the morning, she arrived at Peter's house, where his eyebrows looked up from his paper to her voice.

"Last night..." she started.

His eyes moved to the bruise on her arm.

"I don't want to do anything today." She paused. "This guy grabbed me. He told me to tell you that you should not blow the whistle on something. I cannot be involved in this stuff anymore."

"You'll be all right. I will take care of it," he said, trying to reassure her. "Today is just a picnic, and I'll be there." He momentarily looked at her blank expression. "Slip away. Get into the study. Find anything you can — papers, notes, even a calendar." His hand brushed the air. "Simple."

Ariel sighed a few hours later over a plate dressed in cucumber salad and grilled chicken. Kids were running over the manicured lawn while voices clanged over games of pall-mall and quieted around chess tables scattered throughout the medieval-themed garden party. She was ready to finish this job and turn in her resignation.

"The cards have been calling to you ever since you stood next to the table," a woman's voice said, ladened with a Spanish accent. It momentarily diverted Ariel's attention to the curtain-draped booth. The woman's eyes glistened like sequins against the dark buccaneer garb.

"Come, sit." She spoke with an invitation. "For a moment."

Ariel shook her head, just wanting to get the day over with.

"You can stand there, and I will read the cards. They are dying to talk to you," she said while flipping several over.

Ariel made a quarter turn to face the woman. The food on her plate had not lightened in amount. It all just sat there like a prop. "Go ahead," Ariel said, humoring the woman, biding time.

"The cards want you to know that what they say now is not necessarily for today; there is no timeline, and no date is specified. I will read them after they are all named. Hagalaz. Gebo. Kenaz." Was it Ariel, or did the woman's voice move to echo like a breeze in the branches of trees?

"Kenaz." The sound of the word dripped like honey from the comb, dripping into warm tea. The woman continued, "Secrets may unfold for you over the course of years. Bit by bit you will uncover clues to connections lost.

"Gebo. The secrets will further open the door to this existing generosity, the balance, many people will be touched by the lost connections. Although, it seems you will keep the source secret; you will keep it safe." The words swirled into a whirlpool as she followed with the last card.

"Hagalaz. There are events bringing you to your knees. Such destruction right now cannot be imagined. It's wrath sudden and cataclysmic." The woman abruptly stopped speaking, turning the face of the cards to hide on the table, and withdrew her attention from Ariel.

"Thank you," Ariel said, putting her plate on an empty table. Around her, the echoing laughter from children darting across the lawn, and the mist of conversations evaporated into the late afternoon sky. She shifted her blouse, wincing as her fingers brushed the colorful bruise beneath.

Slipping through the French doors, Ariel let her gaze adjust to the dimmer interior. Sun-warmed terracotta tiles cooled her steps, and the faint scent of lemon furniture polish lingered in the air. Wrought-iron chandeliers hung from the ceiling.

In the study, sunlight drenched the room, drifting in through tall windows, the beams fractured by heavy bookshelves brimmed with tomes. Despite its opulence it was an unsentimental workspace. Ariel's eyes darted to the bare desk, save for a lamp.

Peter's words came to stand next to her: "Simple. Slip away, get into the study, and find something—anything—that ties him to the shipments."

Ariel knew better than to expect carelessness from a man rumored to be a smuggler. Her fingers trembled slightly as she slipped on her gloves, knowing by now leaving prints behind was not an option.

She opened the drawer. Receipts, ledgers, a few pens—all innocuous. But the leather-bound notebook tucked inside an interior drawer caught her attention. Ariel carefully lifted it free, flipping open its cover.

Her fingers steady despite the tension coiled in her chest. The pages lay bare before her, ink etched in deliberate strokes—neat but hurried. Her eyes locked on the text, and the act of seeing became something more. It wasn't a choice, not a skill she had honed. It simply was.

She didn't read the words. She took them. Each page was absorbed in its entirety, precise and whole: the jagged loops of the handwriting, the tilt of the letters, the indentation of a heavy hand pressing pen to paper. The numbers lined up like soldiers in her mind, their meaning unclear but their arrangement impossible to forget. Had she tried to read them, the words may have started dancing across the page, disappearing. But taking the pages, and her surroundings, as a picture was embedded.

She turned the page. Her mind clicked again. The columns

of codes—dense and unbroken—settled into place within her. The faint smudge of ink at the bottom corner. A light crease running down the edge where the page had been dog-eared and then straightened.

Turn. Another page. Her focus sharpened, cold and mechanical. She blinked once, her breath slow and measured.

Ah-ha. I bet that will be helpful. She thought, seeing the sketch of a logo drawn on its side. The drawing was crude but recognizable, a telltale sign of a specific shipping company Peter had mentioned before.

Footsteps tapped their approach, taunted from down the hall. Heavy — deliberate. She slid the notebook back into place, eased the drawers shut, and ripped off her gloves. The rush of blood in her veins moved her like the wind through the door where her path was blocked by a tall, wiry man.

"Looking for something?"

Ariel forced a smile, clutching her hands together, trying to still their shaking. "No, I was just looking for the bathroom. Got a little lost, but the library shelves stopped me, they're beautiful."

His gaze lingered, tracing her face. "Down the hall to your left."

"Thank you," she replied, and walked away with measured steps, counting them in her mind, resisting the urge to run. Only once she slipped out the side door into the fresh air, did she let herself breathe again.

Later that evening, in Peter's office, Ariel was ready to hand in more than just the recently retrieved material which she'd written down for him.

"Peter." Her voice cracked.

"Ariel, great timing. There is someone I want you to meet." Peter pointed to a young man whose sharp jaw and dark, tousled hair gave him the look of an ancient Roman carved from marble, in a pair of jeans. "This is Stuart. You two are going to be working on a few projects together."

Ariel looked at Stuart, whose eyes prickled her lungs. She straightened her shoulders, cleared her throat, and said, "Peter, I really need to talk to you." Her glance bounced between the men.

"Can it wait for a few minutes? I want to go over some things with the two of you," he asked.

She thought, drew her breath, and said, "No. It cannot wait. I'm quitting to find other work." There was no reaction to her announcement. Peter just looked at her, so she said, "I don't want to be making people so upset that they are approaching me at the gas station, stuffing me into their car, and threatening your family or me."

Peter shook his head. "That's taken care of, Ariel. It won't happen again. You have my word."

"No, I need to be done," she said, standing her ground.

Noticing uncertainty play in her fingertips, Stuart looked toward Peter, who spoke with a slow nod. "Understood. Ariel, you have been a great help to me, and I wish you well."

Ariel looked around skeptically, then stepped forward, handing over the latest retrieval.

"Really?"

"Really," Peter said.

"Oh, thank you, Peter. I guess this is it then." Relief blossomed like spring in her chest. "Thank you. For everything." She turned to leave, only for Stuart to casually step in her path.

"Seriously?"

"Yeah, why quit now? With me, you won't be going about things alone. That's why Peter called me. Isn't it, Pete?"

"That's right. And the next project was one I thought you'd find quite intriguing. And not dangerous. Well, not too dangerous, as long as you don't step on any snakes," Peter told her.

"Snakes? Nope." She sounded resolute, at least she thought she did, but curiosity decided to ask, "Where would I have been stepping on snakes?"

"South and Central America," Peter replied. "But don't worry about it now. You should get going. Stuart and I have some planning to do." He was playing coy and knew it was working.

"What would I be doing down there?" she asked.

"*We?* Don't you mean we? What would we be doing down there? From what I hear, it doesn't sound like we, though." Stuart corrected her. "But, I'll be looking for a very specific variety of cacao."

A smile slinked in behind her eyes at the word cacao.

Peter continued, "I have a client looking for a plantation or some cacao tree. More like he is searching for a myth. All you have to do is do a little research. Nothing more than that. Just let me know what you find out."

"That's it, chocolate?" Her curiosity now met skepticism. *There must be a catch they are not telling me about. A ploy to get me down there, to happen upon one of their client's subjects of interest. Another investment investigation, money laundering, something other than that.*

"Chocolate," Peter said.

Chapter Three

An obscure yet profound trait of cocoa lies in its layers of complexity—hidden flavors and notes that only reveal themselves through patience, curiosity, and a willingness to go beyond the surface. The deeper one delves into knowledge or experience, the richer and more nuanced it becomes, just as chocolate's subtleties emerge only when savored slowly.

***

Damion leaned back in his seat, the turbulence rattling his water bottle on the tray table in front of him.

"So," he said, glancing at me, "what happened?"

"She walked onto the plane," I said simply, pausing as another bout of turbulence jolted the cabin.

Damion shook his head, letting out a soft laugh. "That's quite a shift from quitting her job to getting on the plane. And for chocolate?" The flight attendant came by, picking up empty bottles of water, Damion drained his quickly then relinquished the bottle. "So, did the journey prove worth it? Did they find what they were looking for?"

"Well. Let's see."

***

1990

Ariel scanned the room, "We doesn't sound... so bad." And with that statement, curiosity elbowed whatever catch there could've been out the window.

Peter booked them first-class from San Diego to San Francisco and then into Panama. The thick humid air that most people imagine of places surrounded by jungles and rainforests was there to greet them as they disembarked from the plane. Grabbing her small duffle bag, Ariel and Stuart got through customs and found their driver and guide for the first part of their trip.

"Welcome to Panama. You are ready?" He asked, holding open the door of a white Toyota Land Cruiser that would be taking them into the rainforest. It was a winding nine-hour drive to the first village community of Río Oeste Afuera. Their driver pointed out trees and plants typical of the area and gave them the region's history.

The next morning, refreshed from travel, Ariel met Stuart for breakfast.

"So, what do you know about this man who wants the chocolate?" She poured coffee into a small mug. "And, seriously, this is all we are doing down here?"

"The money he's offering is good, and what Pete told me is this guy has been on the hunt for a specific cacao variety for almost twenty years." Stuart explained.

"No, there is something else. This isn't all he is after. There has to be more. I wonder why this guy has thought about this chocolate all this time. The people Peter works with rarely, if ever, do anything without an ulterior motive. At least from what I've seen." It crossed Ariel's mind for a moment that she had also been secretly dreaming of cocoa for the whole of her of life. "And aside from saying it is special and all but extinct, what is he after?"

"Personally, I think the guy is now sixty, has a lot of money, and wants to be part of some mystery. Supposedly he tasted some of this mysterious substance before and has never had the like since. He's trying to find out if it was pure imagination or if there was something to it," Stuart said.

"So, he's been looking for this since, like, 1971? And he hasn't found it in all that time?" Ariel asked. "There is something else. My gut is screaming with conspiracy."

Stuart observed Ariel for a moment. Innocence radiated from her like the softness of sunlight filtering through the canopy upon her shoulders. At the same time, there were burn marks hidden, deep, like the sun's invisible spectrum. While contemplating this, he said, "Well, you heard Pete; the guy had some chocolate amidst a little sexy soiree. The magic of the moment might have been confused . . . maybe he confused it with the sex. So, I am guessing this guy is getting older and wants to taste his prime once more."

After breakfast, they were driven to the head of a bush trail and walked them into the forest. Rocks and roots helped them keep their feet dry from the thick mud that coated the trail. The roots of the rainforest trees were shallow, twisting above the ground, making almost perfect natural stairs for the slippery hills.

"Watch out!" Stuart exclaimed while jumping back, practically knocking into Ariel.

If it were possible to levitate and stay there she would have. But instead, she was frozen in place, not knowing what to do or where to go. Her pulse however repeated, "a snake, a snake. A snake!"

Stuart stood staring at the ground in front of him. "Look at that. I stepped right next to it," His voice shaking, pointing at an almost invisible snake about two feet long, thinnish, camouflaged in olive green with an overlay of long, dark, irregular crossing bands, blocking their path.

Their guide, with a machete in hand, in one fluid movement, hurled the snake deep into the bushes.

Nervously, Ariel looped her thumbs beneath the straps of her backpack, inhaling as if it were her first breath.

"You *are* afraid of snakes," Stuart noted. His rugged exterior softened, seeing her frozen in fear. "Come on. It'll be okay. They don't want to see you as much as you don't want to see them and will, more often than not, move away to avoid you."

"Okay," she said, breathing deeply. "I'm glad I have high boots on anyway, just in case."

"Yes, it's a good thing," he said, smiling. "Just in case."

Over the next few weeks, they became more comfortable navigating the forests, watching where they stepped, where they put their hands, how to store their clothes, and how to shake everything before putting them on in the morning. They were even more comfortable taking small strolls alone here and there.

Early one morning, Ariel was awoken by a soft knocking at the door and a loud whisper. "Ariel, wake up."

"What?" Ariel said sleepily. "What's going on?"

"Get dressed," Stuart whispered a bit louder. "I want to show you something. I'll meet you out here."

The day was waking up. Ariel blinked a few times, focusing in the bright morning light. "What's going on?" she asked again.

"Come on," Stuart said, leading her by the hand momentarily. This was the first time he had done that, touched her so casually. "Before we leave here, I wanted to get a few pictures in this light."

Together they trekked through the rainforest, Ariel pointing out colorful birds, the different blossoms and stopped every so often to breathe-in their heady scents. And of course she watched out for snakes.

Deeper into the forest the air cooled, greeting them with a waterfall plunging into a pool with a grace that belied its powerful descent.

Stuart leaned over a natural log railing where Ariel was silently pointing to the bright blue morpho butterflies.

They had been on this expedition for about a month. A month on the hunt for an elusive cacao, traversing through dense underbrush and over steep ridges. Day after day, they'd woken to the chorus of the jungle, air thick with the promise of discovery. And, in this moment, the rest of the world vanished. Stuart stood, focusing his camera on one of the butterflies, who, unaware of its audience, flitted from leaf to leaf.

"Too bad we can't see this photo until we return." He spoke

into the air. "It could be the best one yet."

"You could get a Polaroid," Ariel suggested lightly, still leaning against the log, eyes blurring everything in a trance-like state except for the vibrant blue wings. "I wish we could stay here, just for a little longer," she said. Stuart looked up from his camera. Ariel followed his gaze and noted, "Your eyes are the same color as the butterfly's wings."

"Wow, that's pretty bright. I've been told lighting can change the shade of blue they are," he said, stepping closer to look at her eyes. "And your eyes look like"—he looked around,—"like the earth by the pool. Hazel with a little . . ." He looked closer before she shifted her glance to the floor.

"You mean they look like dirt?" Ariel said, quickly simplifying his description, remembering what others had told her before about her eyes, that they were dull, and the color of shit. Although she did not hear him mirror those sentiments, she also didn't want to give him the chance to do so. She wanted to keep feeling as she had been, melded into the forest.

Stuart's face was so close to hers that when she glanced up, she had no time to find an exit. She had no time to think before his lips were on hers.

Closing her eyes, she slipped into the jungle, though her body remained motionless. His lips brushed hers—tender. Oh no. Oh no. A pulse of panic drummed beneath her skin. Someone would see. Someone would know. But he was so untroubled, his ease seeping into her like sunlight through dense leaves, coaxing something delicate to unfurl. A quiet ache pushed past her fear, reaching for the light. Tentatively, she placed her hands on his shoulders, drawing nearer, yearning for the impossible—to dissolve, to drift weightless, if only for the space between the butterfly's wings.

His hand moved to the small of her back.

And that's when they came—monsters draped in familiar voices, slithering from the shadows, their whispers pierced as thorns. They coiled around her, twisting tight, creeping like ivy with teeth, choking out the air, the warmth, the light.

"He doesn't really like you, does he? How could he? No one can."

Ariel flinched. The ancient echoes embedded in her bones. Always waited for the perfect moment to remind her. The jeering laughter, sharp as broken glass.

"What is wrong with you? You fraud... he is going to find out about you. And you will ruin his life too."

The forest pressed in. The trees loomed, their twisted branches curling away from her in quiet disgust. Leaves shuddered, whispering the truth she could never escape. The grass beneath her feet recoiled. Even the flowers—vibrant moments ago—wilted in her presence. The whole world watched, bearing silent witness to her fraudulence.

"*I know, I know I am not good.*" Her mind answered back. "*I'll stop. Please. Stop.*"

The moment with Stuart fractured, slipping through her fingers like water. "*How dare you touch him? How dare you.*"

She wanted to shrink into herself, to hide. But there was nowhere to go.

"*You should be ashamed of yourself.*"

"We can't." Now, words fell from her lips, barely above a whisper, as her hands, those hesitant arbiters, pressed against Stuart's chest. A plea for understanding cloaked in the guise of restraint.

"Okay," he said, his voice steady, a lifeline offered in the gentle sea of rejection. "It's okay."

The weeks that followed found their relationship evolving into an exploration of its own. Subtle shifts in conversation, the quiet gravity of knowing someone without needing to fill the space between words. In the final week of their expedition, they found themselves sharing a single room, where the lines between friendship and something more blurred—but never fully crossed.

Ariel tugged a blanket higher over her lap, its soft alpaca

wool brushing against her fingers. The air smelled of rain-soaked earth and wood smoke from the nearby huts.

Beside her, Stuart set his tea onto the coffee table and sat down. He didn't speak right away, just leaned back into the worn cushions, stretching his legs out in front of him. He had a way of settling into a moment without demanding anything from it, letting the quiet expand rather than pressing into it with unnecessary words.

Ariel exhaled slowly, her gaze drifting to the open window where the last hints of light bled into the trees. Her hands twisted the edge of the blanket in her lap, an unconscious movement, a tether to something safe.

"I can hear you thinking," Stuart murmured.

A small, tired smile flickered at the corner of her lips. "Is it that obvious?"

She risked a glance at him, finding nothing but quiet amusement in his expression. No pressure. No expectation. Just patience.

He let the silence stretch between them again, giving her space to fill it or leave it empty.

Ariel turned the cup of tea in her hands, watching the steam curl into the cool night air. "I'm not good at this," she admitted.

"At drinking tea?" he teased lightly.

She huffed a soft laugh, shaking her head. "No. At... being in the same room."

"Our little hut has two bedrooms. It is okay, Ariel."

"I mean... well... letting people close."

Stuart didn't react right away. He just nodded. Then, after a moment, said, "You don't have to be."

The simplicity of it unsettled her. But Stuart just sat there, waiting, letting her unfold in her own time.

Ariel glanced at him again, searching for something—some sign of frustration, impatience, disappointment. But all she found was that same steady patience, like a gentle tide meeting the shore, never rushing, never demanding.

Her focus moved to the mug in her hands, the way her fingers curled around it. The warmth seeping into her palms, a quiet comfort.

"I just... don't know what to do with this," she said, so softly she wasn't sure he even heard her.

Stuart leaned forward slightly, resting his forearms on his knees, but he didn't close the space between them. "Then don't do anything."

Ariel frowned, glancing up.

"You don't have to figure it out right now," he said simply.

"Or ever, if that's what feels right. I'm not asking for anything."

"But, back in the forest... a few weeks ago."

"Do you remember how the blue butterfly rested upon the flowers? How simple it was? How natural?"

She nodded.

"Ariel, when I kissed you, it wasn't to capture you or force it into anything. I kissed you because, to me, you were just as beautiful as the butterfly."

Was it disbelief that flushed her cheeks—or fear? No, it was more like something dangerously close, to relief.

She swallowed, nodding once, then shifted slightly, allowing the blanket to fall just enough to brush against his arm. A small, almost imperceptible movement, but Stuart noticed. He didn't call attention to it, didn't move closer or pull away. He just let it happen.

A strand of Ariel's hair fell loose, catching in a gentle breeze. Stuart moved without hesitation, his fingers tucking it behind her ear. When she didn't shy away, he reached out again. brushing her hand—and Ariel watch him touch her.

He leaned in, checking the boundaries in her eyes, before continuing to place his lips upon hers.

The kiss was light. Questioning. But it grew in confidence

as she responded, her hands coming up to rest on his shoulders. The hidden voices of her father and siblings fell away; there was only the two of them now, and the whisper of their movements.

"Come with me," Stuart took her hand, guiding her. She couldn't say no, not that she wanted to. Her body moved on its own, allowing him to lay her down against the simple linens that dressed the bed, allowing him to remove her own. Exposing her to his touch.

***

In their final days, they ventured into Venezuela to taste the rare jewel of cocoa. The air in Porcelana was thick with the scent of possibility, mingled with the faint sweetness of cocoa fermenting nearby. The sun dipped low, casting a honeyed glow over the dense canopy of trees that bordered the plantation. Ariel stepped cautiously out of the weathered Land Cruiser, her boots crunching against the gravel drive as her eyes scanned the scene.

Rows of cocoa trees stretched out before her, their gnarled trunks bending under the weight of the history they carried. The fruit hung heavy, a palette of pale yellows and soft greens, their hues more delicate than the bold purples and oranges she had seen on other plantations. These pods were subtle, refined, nature had crafted them with the precision of an artist painting in pastels.

"So, this is it," Stuart said, as he hoisted his camera strap higher on his shoulder. He was already in motion, his steps deliberate as he approached the nearest tree. "Porcelana. The rarest of the rare."

Ariel followed, her curiosity in quiet wonder. "It doesn't look like much," she said softly, brushing her fingertips against the bark of a nearby trunk.

"That's part of the mystery," Stuart replied.

Ariel ran her fingers over a pod. "These trees were almost wiped out in the late-nineteenth century. Disease, neglect . . . they were forgotten, left to vanish while other varieties like Forastero dominated the market. But here, in this corner of Venezuela, they held on. Barely." Her attention was drawn to a nearby worker who cracked open a pod with practiced ease. The exposed beans were startlingly pale, nearly white, glistening with pulp.

The plantation owner approached, his weathered face breaking into a warm smile as he extended his hand. "Bienvenidos," he said, his voice carrying the rich cadence of a storyteller. "Welcome to our little piece of history."

Stuart and Ariel introduced themselves, and the man led them to a shaded table where small cups of cocoa awaited. "Taste," he urged, his smile growing as he watched their reactions.

Ariel lifted the cup to her lips, the dark liquid sliding over her tongue like velvet. It was unlike any chocolate she had ever tasted—smooth and complex, with layers that unfolded in waves. She caught hints of dried apricot, a trace of roasted hazelnut, followed by something deeper, almost smoky. It was intoxicating.

"Is this what he's been searching for?" she murmured, her thoughts trailing to the client who had sent them here, to the myths and dreams he had woven around what he tasted all those years before.

Stuart nodded, savoring his own sip. "This is amazing," he said after a long pause. "It's... Every note, every layer . . . all wrapped up in this one fragile bean."

"This," Ariel said finally, setting her cup down, "this was worth the journey."

***

"So," Damion said, shifting in his seat, "was it the cacao the guy was looking for?"

His question stirred a few others around us. I caught the way his fingers hovered near his duffle bag, the parchment-wrapped chocolate inside.

"At the time, they all thought it was," I said. "And for a while, they let themselves believe the mystery had been solved. But when Ariel stepped off that plane coming home in 1990 with cacao in her hands the more questions about the cacao took root."

The plane bounced, jarring a distinguished-looking man from the center row. The man bearing an uncanny resemblance to Henry Kissinger, leaned toward me. "Excuse me," he said, voice gravel-thick, "don't mean to pry, but you're saying the quest for this mysterious chocolate wasn't resolved? And what about the man in the parking lot? What was that all about?"

I exhaled, stretching my fingers against the armrest.

"That's a good question," I said. "The truth? Ariel never learned what truly caused that confrontation in the parking lot. But I have my suspicion and will tell you in bit."

The Kissinger look-alike tilted his head slightly, waiting.

Madge, the flight attendant, who had been following the conversation between rounds of serving drinks, folded her arms and leaned against the galley wall. "Did she find it, the chocolate?" she asked. "And what about Stuart? What happened between them?"

That was the question, wasn't it?

"Well," I said slowly, "They stayed close. Neither of them ever quite defined what that closeness was. Not really. The few days of the cacao trip there was intimacy. It seemed natural, inevitable."

I paused. "But it wasn't the right direction for them."

Damion frowned. "So, it just… ended?"

"Not exactly," I said. "Because those few nights together, gifted them. And, nine months later David was born."

A few murmurs passed through the listeners.

"And then the second time, she asked him directly," I continued. "She wanted David to have a sibling. So, she asked."

Madge's brows lifted. "And he said yes?"

"Yes." I said simply. "And soon after, Gresham was born." I took a sip of water. "Stuart never claimed the title of father, but he was always there. Even when the world around them changed, even when Ariel made choices that pulled her in different directions, he remained her friend."

Madge tilted her head. "How many kids did she have?"

"Three sons," I said.

Her lips pursed slightly. "Was the third… Stuart's?"

"No," I said. "A few years after Gresham was born, she turned to a friend. A nuclear engineer she had met during her deep dive into quantum mechanics…"

"Same arrangement as Stuart?" he had asked, adjusting his glasses.

"Yes. No expectations, no complications. Just…" She hesitated, searching for the words. "I've been thinking about it, and I do—I want one more child. I know you like kids, so I thought... maybe?"

He had studied her for a long moment.

"We don't have to do anything... I mean, do anything... intimate. You know."

"And that's how Brandon, her youngest son came to be. Three sons, each brought into the world in their own way. And each of them grew up by Ariel's side, chasing adventures the way she always had."

Madge moved to do an aisle check only to ask on return, "And Stuart?"

I glanced past Damion to the window, watching the scattered clouds.

"They remained friends, until the end."

Chapter Four

2008

The piece of chocolate crumbled slightly as Ariel unwrapped it, the bloom ghosting across its surface like frost. It had been with her for years—part relic, part question.

Eighteen years since the expedition with Stuart.

And still, the answer had never come.

Around her, the house displayed quiet signs of obsession: stacks of books on pre-Columbian trade, maps of West Africa pinned beside cocoa-stained recipe cards, samples labeled in black ink with names only she could decipher.

Ariel reached for her notebook and began sketching figures—financials, travel timelines, crop yields. Pages layered like sediment, the past pressing into the present.

She paused. Her pencil stilled.

I can afford to take time off.

The phone call to Peter lasted less than a minute. He didn't ask questions, only said, "Just come back to us."

By spring, the world of cacao had overtaken the house.

In the kitchen, David flipped a cocoa bean between his fingers, Gresham scanned a field guide, and Brandon traced invisible glyphs into the dust near the hearth.

They didn't notice her watching—didn't see the way she quietly studied them, thankful for their little family.

She didn't have to gather them or announce anything. She simply opened the drawer beneath the sink, pulled out three manila folders, and laid them on the table. Each was labeled in her hand:

Volta Region–Ghana

Fermentation Practices

Safari Logistics

The boys looked up.

The house stood on tiptoes, floorboards attempting to peer over the counter with them.

That was all it took.

Brandon's notebook snapped shut.

David leaned in.

Gresham smiled.

Ariel poured a cup of cocoa and stood by the window. The house stilled beside her.

"Ghana. What do you guys say? Then the International Cocoa Conference."

***

After three months in the Volta Region, the red dust of Ghana still clung to their boots and the backs of their necks as they made their way to Bali.

Here, the jungle's wild pulse gave way to polished glass and the vocabulary of global commodity.

Outside the keynote hall, Ariel followed the boys as they wandered through the maze of exhibition booths. She'd expected Ghana to change them—but not this much.

David paused beside a German booth labeled Post-Fermentation Drying Optimization.

He listened, brow furrowed, as a woman explained a solar drying system.

"Do you find consistency issues in the rainy season?" he asked. "Or do you have backup protocols for humidity spikes?"

The woman blinked. "You've worked in cocoa?"

David shook his head. "Just learning."

A few booths over, Gresham thumbed through a booklet on soil pH ranges for Theobroma cacao. A French botanist leaned in to hear his question.

"Et... estce que vous pensez que la qualité du sol influence plus le goût, ou la résistance aux maladies?"(Do you think soil quality affects taste more—or disease resistance?)

The botanist laughed softly. "Good French. To answer your question, both."

Brandon lingered near a video loop of beans being turned in wooden boxes.

"Do you think the shape of the box affects the flavor?" he asked.

The exhibitor frowned. "The shape?"

"Yeah. If corners trap heat or cool faster than the center... wouldn't that change the microbial balance?"

The man winked, then smiled. "Maybe you should be giving the presentation."

Ariel drifted to a table lined with transparent containers of origin samples—each labeled with altitude, variety, and harvest month.

A hand reached for the same container she was examining—D.R. Congo, 510m altitude, Trinitario hybrid.

"Sorry," said the man beside her, pulling back with a faint smile. "Go ahead."

She looked up.

His badge read: Jim Backlish — Attorney / Private Consultant.

He had the mild, unassuming look of a man who could vanish into any crowd.

"No worries," she said.

He nodded toward the sample. "You think terroir really matters in cocoa—or are we just borrowing too much from the wine world?"

"I think..." she hesitated, fingers brushing the jar, "the land remembers more than we give it credit for."

"You've been to origin?"

"Just back from Ghana."

He gave a low whistle. "That's the real classroom."

He offered his hand. "Jim."

"Ariel."

"Nice to meet you."

"What flavor notes are you after?" he asked.

She didn't answer right away. "I guess I'm just curious to see what's out there," she said softly. "I kind of have a fairytale in mind."

"A fairytale?" He smiled. "That's new for this crowd. What's yours?"

"A childhood memory," she said, her eyes on the samples. "My father gave me a piece of chocolate once. It was small, but it stayed. Maybe because it was the first. Maybe because it was from him. Either way—it started something."

Jim nodded, turning slightly toward the lecture hall. "Not many people can trace their obsession to a single bite. Good luck in your search."

Inside the keynote room, Ariel and the boys sat with notebooks open, waiting.

Jim appeared again, this time with a small paper cup of cocoa tea.

"Mind if I sit?"

She shook her head.

They sat in companionable quiet, the air steeped in roasted sweetness.

"My employer sent me here hoping I'd find a fairytale," Jim

said after a moment. "Not really a cocoa guy myself, but I've been coming for years."

Ariel tilted her head. "Does he have a favorite?"

He gave a half-smile. "Yeah. A cocoa that doesn't officially exist."

Her fingers tightened on her own cup of tea.

He didn't notice.

"He had an experience years ago," Jim continued. "Life-changing, he says. Involving a woman." He gave a short, embarrassed laugh. "Sounds ridiculous, I know. But he's spent nearly four decades chasing it—rumors, lost fermentations, jungle strains. Every year, I show up, listen to panels, sip samples, and hope someone drops a name."

"Found anything?" she asked.

"Nothing real," Jim said. "But that's the thing about fairytales—they aren't real. Sorry to say. I know you've got your own one."

Ariel's heart moved inside her chest like a slow-turning key.

She sipped her cocoa tea, steady.

"Would he ever hire an investigations firm to track leads?" she asked lightly.

Jim chuckled. "Wouldn't surprise me. He never drops a thread once he's pulled it."

She didn't blink.

Said nothing of Stuart.

Nothing of Peter.

Nothing of the jungle that almost swallowed her in 1990.

"Well," she said quietly, "I hope he finds what he's looking for."

Jim raised his cup. "Same to you."

The room settled. The first slide of the keynote flickered to life.

For a moment, the air between them held a stillness too complete to be coincidence.

Even the cocoa samples on the nearby table seemed to lean closer—listening.

***

"Excuse me." Damion reached across me and touched Madge's hand.

"Yes?" The color of her cheeks brightened.

"Do you have any pretzels?" he asked.

"Sure," she said, pulling a packet from her apron pocket.

As Damion opened the small foil packet, I sipped on some sparkling water. "If you don't mind, I'd like to step back a moment back in time."

Harvey, a.k.a. "Kissinger," patted his chest after a shot of Jack Daniel's. "Let's hear it," he said, restraining an air bubble in his chest. "The history."

"Okay, here goes. Ariel's biological father was a shrewd businessman, publicly patient, but privately unforgiving."

Chapter Five

His name was Edward Burke, and his sights were focused. Determination coursed relentlessly through his veins. Power pulsed through his body, producing a constant flow of natural morphine; his high was interrupted only by his wife's complaints—He worked too much! She never saw him! And, by early 1971, he'd had enough of her bitching.

His private secretary, Mary, peered through the partially open door of his office before going home, checking for any last work. He was on the phone at his desk, running his fingers over the polished mahogany, tracing the grain. Looking up, he caught her eyes, signaling her to wait with the lift of a finger. Known for having an authoritative demeanor and an inherent ability to stay calm in a storm, he was clearly trying to control his voice while arguing with his wife, pausing to listen, attempting to agree.

"Yes, Elizabeth, if you think it is for the best"—he paused again and took a deep breath. "We will work through this. You are right; it is important." He listened for a moment longer before sitting abruptly upright, raising his voice but still in control. "For Christ's sake, Elizabeth, stop being so dramatic. What's done is done."

There was a long pause. Mary started walking away from the door to gather her things. His voice was muffled in the hallway. Despite her better judgment, Mary consciously strained to make out what he was saying. Barely audible, she heard Burke wind down the exchange with a suddenly honey-coated voice, the tone he used to close a deal.

"A few months away will be good for everybody," he insisted. "Yes, we will talk. I said we would. Just not right now. I have too much going on. Besides, you like California."

The sound of the receiver being set down echoed in the now-empty offices. Mary had already lifted her cardigan off the coat rack when he called, "Mary?"

"Yes?"

With the sweater over her arm, she returned to his office doorway. He'd recently been talking with her, venting about his life, after hours. She listened more than spoke, thinking there was nothing she could actually say that would help, as she had no genuine experience in things of this nature. After all, she'd just turned nineteen, and he was forty.

According to the gossip, if he wanted something, he got it. What he couldn't build, he bought. What he couldn't buy, he took. And that was the Edward Burke who unburdened himself to Mary.

She was thankful to have her job, even though subservience hardly fit her natural self, but it was better than her previous foray as a cocktail waitress. Mary carried the best of her petite but fierce dark Irish and French heritage like a queen, coupled with what Edward Burke apparently saw as her nurturing nature, which he began to confide in freely. She sensed this and knew to tread lightly when staying after hours so as not to confuse or interfere with her job.

"Thanks for sticking around," he said.

She shrugged from the doorway, studying the blue Picasso figurines on the bookshelves. "There was some paperwork that needed filing."

"Mary," he said as she stared inquiringly, "you know how much I appreciate your dedication, don't you?" His question seemed to carry much greater weight than a simple compliment about her office work.

"I need to head out, Mr. Burke. Is there something you need?" Mary asked.

He cocked an eyebrow. "No. I'll see you in the morning."

"Good night then, Mister Burke."

Three days passed with a strange sense of heightened awareness between them. Each comment bore a double entendre, each moment an electrically fueled dance of the mundane. Brief physical contact—the press of his hand here, a teasing grasp there—appeared innocent at a glance yet cloaked deeper feelings that she found were almost unbearable. Of course, such behavior would go nowhere today. It was a different time back then.

And being so much younger than he was, her experience in the ways of the world was limited, but she was not completely naive. She didn't dwell in the la-la land of Hollywood make-believe; nakedly innocent, she had experienced magnificent ecstasy with her last boyfriend, Benny, whom she still saw periodically.

In truth, she found the current adventure bracing, fun, and exciting enough to make it just a tad dangerous. If others in the office noticed anything different about her relationship with Burke, they kept it to themselves. The world was the same, boring in every way, except how the two of them moved through it.

One evening she gathered her things to go home and brought a needed file into Burke's office.

"Is there anything else?" she asked, placing it on the desk.

He sat on the leather couch, bathed in the orange glow of a table lamp as he read through a stack of reports. He glanced up. The lamplight illuminated him in a kind of firelight that might have aroused a lesser female, and, indeed, her ego shuttered slightly, for he was admittedly a handsome man. His eyes smouldered as he looked at her.

"No, that will be... You know, Elizabeth and I have officially separated. It's over." He paused, never taking his steely eyes off her.

"I'm sorry to hear that. Is there anything I can do?"

"No," he said, letting the report in his hand fall to the couch. "On second thought, why don't you make me a scotch."

"Sure, Mister Burke."

Gliding across the palace-sized Persian rug in his office to the bar on the bookcase, Mary held, somewhat protectively, to the handbag she carried under her arm. Her heart followed a rhythm of an ancient dance, moving with instinct. A small glass rubbed between her palms at the bar, adding heat before she poured the pure, amber-colored liquor. Artfully she opened the handbag, removing a small parchment-lined box. Ever so carefully, she unveiled finely ground cocoa beans and added a pinch of the dark powder to the drink. She moved smoothly, as though following choreography she'd known since the day she was born. The orange glow of the lamp slowed time as the glass moved to him, a sacrifice to a god.

When he touched her fingers, electricity sparked. Standing uncertainly, she watched him bring the glass to his lips. Liquid slid down his throat; lips leisurely brought the powder into his mouth. He raised his eyes.

Although clothed, she'd never felt more naked in her entire life. Shifting weight from right to left, she longed to taste the cocoa-enhanced scotch in his mouth.

He placed his hands firmly behind her thighs, just below the hem of her skirt. Her knees trembled, easing her one step closer. The scent of the scotch mingled with his cologne, and just a hint of perspiration sent a bolt of electricity right through her chest.

A sharp breath escaped as his hands slid up the back of her thighs, pushing the hem of her skirt, teasing the bands of her thigh-high nylons. And stopped against the smooth, tight cotton of her panties.

She lowered her mouth to his, gently taking in his lower lip. Upon tasting the rich, residual cocoa, she feared for a second that she might faint. His hands traced a path beneath her skirt, drawing her close as warmth pooled in the spaces between them. He pulled her into his arms, lifting her effortlessly before carrying her to the desk.

* * *

As we were about to continue, the woman sitting in front of Damion tilted her seat back until we could see her face framed by peppered streaks of hair similar to mine, only more frizzled.

"Hi," she said, maneuvering her arm over to wave. "I have a confession to make. I've been eavesdropping on your story."

"Oh? I can stop if the story is bothering you," I told her.

"Actually, would you mind talking just a tiny bit louder?" she asked.

"Sure," I said.

"Thank you. My name is Melony Hearsom, by the way."

Right upon Melony's confession, Harvey interjected, "Tell me, do you really have someone's ashes in your carry-on? And when is this Greg fellow showing up in this story?"

"Yes, I have ashes with me, and Greg will be along in a bit. But we are still back in the spring of 1971 right now. He shows up quite a bit later in 2010."

"Well, it's a hell of a tale either way." He gazed around, meeting the others' agreement.

"Look at this, we've all gathered around and we're looking for s'more," said Damion, amused by his own attempt at a pun.

"Say, son"—Harvey leaned over me to catch Damion's attention—"just what kind of business are you in?"

"My partner and I have distribution rights for a new Korean optical communications system, kind of like a digital contact lens. It is a recent technology that allows someone to augment vision in such a way that if we were using it now, this story would be able to play out for us as it is being told."

"Oh, bet it's just a fad. Better get out while you can. Technology moves so fast anymore that it is hardly worth the investment. Stick to commodities, I say."

"I'll keep that in mind, thank you." Damion appeased.

"I don't mean to be rude, but I'd really like to hear the next part of your story," interrupted Melony. "Last I heard, he'd swept her up in his arms, heading for his desk."

"The scotch! You're right. The story's hanging in a place where no one really likes to stop, isn't it?" I said, returning to the story.

* * *

Over the course of the next week, the memory of their soirée, infused with the sharp, dark notes of cocoa, thrummed like a secret melody in Edward's mind. By the end of the week it had become too much, and he pulled Mary aside.

"What was in that scotch?" his voice secreted through the office hum.

"Cocoa."

"Cocoa? Anything else?"

"No, I just thought you'd like it after how rough your month has been."

"I want another drink," he demanded quietly, the hunger in his eyes on the verge of starvation. "Tonight."

His whisper brushed her ear as she turned back to her desk.

When the building quieted, thick aromas of chocolate meandered through the corridor. Mary imagined Edward rising from his desk, guided along the hall like an Airedale Terrier, nose erect to the scent. When he did arrive, he found Mary with her back to him, her gentle hourglass figure tightly swathed in a black wrap skirt. She was returning the small cocoa box to her bag.

"Is that it?" he asked, motioning to her purse.

"Yes," she said protectively.

"May I?" He lifted her hand, reaching into the bag. His fingers brushed over the powder, taking a pinch before rubbing it to feel the texture. "Does all chocolate have these effects? Because I've never experienced them. Is there something else in there?"

Mary spoke matter-of-factly, though in her mind it was a purposeful tease, "I'm not too sure."

She smiled in her most impish fashion as she took the box back and closed it like a priceless treasure. "I mean there is nothing else in there besides cocoa. But the story goes, and I am not sure if I'm remembering the story correctly. But from what I do remember, my friend's great-great-great-great—I think that is the right number of greats—grandparents stumbled upon it in their travels through the rainforests, a hundred years ago, like twenty years before Hershey started up in the 1890s." She recounted what she'd been told about the history of the cocoa.

"And your friend's family still gets it?" Looking down at her, he lowered his hands to her hips. While working for Mister Burke, she had already realized that despite his debonair good looks, he would always put business first. And there was excitement in his presence.

"Well, I don't know," she answered with a stumble. "I was given this box and hardly ever eat it. I don't think it was a common plant to begin with. I don't know the whole story. It's more like a fairytale now."

His hands drifted ever so gently around her bottom. She leaned against him, closing her eyes, reciting the story, dreamily ditching the dictionary tone. She breathed in; the small office kitchen now bore the aroma of an ancient ritual. "This is what I was told—" She made up a quick story trying to veer away from the truth. "An ancient people, whose alchemist brewed from this cocoa, was already shrinking. Well, I guess it was more like the tribe was moving out of the area for some reason. Who knows? According to the legend of the people, this cacao dates back almost two thousand years. Then sometime during the Spanish conquests, it was said that cocoa from this particular species was unsuitable for human consumption. Maybe they were protecting something precious because, by that time, cacao cultivation was already taking place and producing more cocoa that the area's people could use for trade with the Spanish. Well, trade in general. I don't know. I am just going off what my friend told me. This strain of cocoa you are tasting moved into the mists, like Avalon."

"How did your friend's ancestors find it?" he asked.

She turned in his arms to stir the dark, simmering liquid.

"Well, okay, this is how my friend's family actually acquired it . . ." Simmering wine curled through the air, mingling with the earthy aroma of the rare cocoa she had carefully measured. Mary stirred the dark mixture, the warmth of the room pressing against her cheeks as she glanced at Edward, who stood just a step too close, his eyes fixed on her. She paused, letting the spoon rest for a moment as she met his curious gaze, aware that his interest was not just romantic but calculated. He was always listening for more than she was willing to share. Her voice became low and lilting.

"A long time ago, in a Sicilian port—a place known for its dark alleys and rough sailors—a man found himself entangled in a life he never chose," she said, eyes drifting trying to remember. "He was a craftsman, humble but sharp, and one night, after saving a merchant from a group of desperate men, he was rewarded not with gold or jewels, but something far stranger."

"What did he receive?"

"A parcel," she said, the word barely a whisper. "Wrapped in cloth, with dark beans inside that carried a scent unlike anything he'd known. The merchant told him, 'Guard these as you would your own life.'" She shifted her weight, the memory of the story threading itself through her mind.

Mary's hand tightened around the edge of the counter as she glanced at Edward, whose eyes had narrowed with intrigue. She chose her next words carefully, skimming over the details that would tie too many threads together. "But these weren't just any beans—they came from a place where the trees grew wild, protected by tribes who knew their worth, who warned that the cocoa was not meant for those who did not understand its story."

Edward leaned forward, close enough that the heat from

the simmering pot warmed both their skin. "And did he guard them?" His voice was a murmur, filled with both wonder and the pursuit of something more tangible.

"He tried," she said softly, stirring the liquid once more. "But life has a way of pulling you in directions you don't expect. The story says that the beans passed through hands, each one less aware of what they held, until their significance was nearly forgotten."

She lifted the spoon, letting the dark, aromatic wine drip back into the pot, and sighed. "And so here we are, drinking something that was meant to be guarded, its secrets lost in the telling."

"What's the real story, Mary?"

She shrugged, wordless, leaning back into his arms.

"Did your friend ever go see these cocoa plants?" Edward asked.

"I don't know. I don't know if they ever traveled there." Mary thought for a moment. "It is interesting that hardly anyone in my friend's extended family knows anything about this; they just aren't that interested. I guess they pretty much humored their grandfather because it was important to him for some reason or another. So, why not play along for a bit? I thought that was sweet; it makes an old man happy. This is all a very brief version of what really happened, I'm sure," Mary tittered leisurely. "I really don't know much about it. It's just a fun story my friend told me, that is all."

Edward considered the story for a moment. "Mary, this friend of yours, is it you?"

Mary was momentarily stunned, then responded quickly, "No, truly. It is not me."

He looked at her incredulously.

"Really." She tried proving to him it wasn't her story without mentioning her ex-boyfriend Benny. "My friend loves telling me stories and gave me this as part of the tale. That's it. I wouldn't take it too seriously, Edward. Truly, it is just a game." She rubbed her temple. "Plus, you can go to the store and get chocolate these days, anyway. That's what my friend probably did." She laughed thinking of Benny coming up with the fantastic story knowing how much she liked mystery novels.

Edward's mind dwelt not on the adventures of what he believed were actually her predecessors but rather dually upon her warming body and the cold, hard facts of an investment opportunity.

"Is it salvageable?" His questions kept coming.

Her shoulders drew up in question. "What? Is what salvageable?"

"Is the plantation where the plants grow—can it be restored?" He worded the question more directly.

"I don't know. I've never been there," she said with a shrug, sending a ribbon of red wine into the mug, infusing the cocoa. "Here, try this."

Even before his first sip, the rising steam offered a taste to Edward's palate. Twenty minutes later, clothing lined the hallway to his office. Mary's legs wrapped around his waist. On the couch, the heat of orgasm radiated.

Edward's lips pressed her ear to form "I love you."

***

"Can we put the story on a quick pause?" asked Damion. "I'd like to stretch my legs for a minute." Intentionally keeping to his side of the aisle so as not to bump into me again, he walked toward the back of the plane.

When Damion took to the aisle, Melony stood next to our seats to stretch. "Did Mary know how Edward was going to respond to the cocoa? Is that why she gave it to him?"

"Well," I said. "Mary didn't fully grasp the extraordinary nature of the cocoa powder when she offered it to Edward. Having led a life filled with uncommon experiences, she had come to see unusual events as part of her normal reality. Perhaps the cocoa's influence blended into what she already assumed of her life, making it easy to overlook.

"So, when she shared it with Edward, I don't believe it was with the intention of creating an intense reaction or seducing him—she simply thought he'd enjoy it. She saw it as a small indulgence, not realizing the cocoa would strike Edward with such force, awakening something deeper in him. His response surprised her, revealing effects she hadn't recognized or understood. It was only in that moment, witnessing Edward's reaction, that Mary began to suspect there might be more to her family's cocoa than she had ever imagined."

Chapter Six

"How was your trip to India? Was it hard to get around out there?" Damion asked, returning from his stroll.

"It was a good trip, peaceful even in the midst of millions of people. You know, Mark Twain once said the place is older than history, older than tradition, older even than legend, and looks twice as old as all of them put together. I landed in Mumbai before heading to Varanasi. There are more than seven hundred miles between the two of them, and the trip is done by ox cart."

"Wait, what?" Damion looked at me with a disbelieving smile. "You're kidding, right?"

"Yes, I'm kidding. I flew. You know, you seem so familiar to me. Strange how people can seem so familiar, isn't it?"

Ignoring the comment, Damion asked, "So, why did Benny give Mary those beans?"

A Simple Twist of Chocolate

I took a breath. "From what I understand, Benny's decision to give Mary the cocoa beans was a mix of both skepticism and hope—a reflection of his complicated relationship with the strange legacy passed down to him by his grandfather.

"Benny grew up with stories that straddled the line between myth and truth, tales told in hushed tones by his grandfather, woven with warnings and mystery. As a pragmatic man forged by the realities of organized crime in Omaha, Benny struggled to believe fully in the fantastical elements of his family's lore. The cocoa, with its whispers of power and sacred history, was something he respected but never truly embraced as anything "That is until Mary. Meeting Mary is when the story began to creep with ivy over the cobblestoned word his grandfather set so many years before. A path leading directly to her, he had no choice but to share it.

"So, he gave her the cocoa beans as a gift.

"No one had given her a gift before, not like this, not with so much meaning.

"That night she looked closely at the beans, turning them over in her hands under the soft light hanging over her kitchen table, she was struck by their almost otherworldly scent. She thought the beans should've lost any scent they had after all those years, but there it was. "it's just a ruse, that the beans were probably new. But why would his grandfather guard the cocoa

80

or make up such a story?" That was the question that gnawed at her.

"One evening, a few weeks later, curiosity took hold. Mary. She laid a few beans on the kitchen counter, grinding them into a fine, dark powder. She mixed the powder into a glass of warm milk, stirred it slowly, then raised the cup to taste.

"Was it heat that spread through her chest, steady and sure, like setting fire to kindling? She didn't have time to follow the sensation further as a knock showed up upon her apartment door.

It came just past midnight.

Three quick knocks.

She crossed the quiet apartment without a word and opened the door.

Benny stood there, rain still beading along the shoulders of his coat. He didn't speak. He didn't need to.

The heat in her chest spread as she ran her hands beneath the wet wool, and kissed him.

His coat slid from his shoulders, pooling on the floor as the world leaned in closer, its edges more defined. Highlighting a world that had never quite followed the ordinary rules.

"As the night wore on, she realized the cocoa wasn't just

a relic or a fairytale; there was something to what Benny had shared. And if that was really the case, she decided to became a keeper of the mystery." I thought for a second. "You might be wondering, then, why she put the powder in Edward's drink."

Damion nodded, and so did a few others.

"Mary added the cocoa powder to Edward Burke's scotch out of curiosity—pure and simple. She had tasted the beans herself, but the experience had left her with more questions than answers. Was it the cocoa, or just her imagination? Could someone else feel it too?

"She had some of the powder she'd ground with her because she had planned to have a friend try it. But when Edward asked her to pour a drink for him, she thought it would be something different, something that may set her apart from the others in his eyes. So, she put a small pinch into the drink. She wasn't nervous about doing it—there was nothing illicit about cocoa, it was just the same as making a cocktail at the bar after all — and it was obvious it was in the drink. Still, as Edward took the glass, she watched with intention as he lifted the glass to his lips and took a slow sip.

"And then, without a word, Edward pulled her toward him. And you know what happened from there."

Damion looked toward his bag and the small, coveted parcel within.

Melony's face appeared over the seat back. "You know, Mary was taking a big chance. I once worked in Atlanta, years ago, where any secretary who slept with her boss was summarily fired without a recommendation. Granted, Mary's fling was during a period of free love." She remained facing over the seat.

"True, but even free love can bring more than expected. Should we continue?" I asked.

A chorus of gentle yesses rose around the cabin.

Just as I drew a breath to continue, Harvey, having a penchant for trivia, leaned in from across the aisle. "Speaking of taking chances," he said, "do you realize that on this flight path from New Delhi to New York, we're crossing over some of the most historically diverse regions on the planet? We'll fly over the Himalayas first, frozen sentinels that have watched over the land for millennia."

Melony raised an eyebrow as Harvey continued. "And after that, we'll skim above the ancient landscapes of Afghanistan and Iran. Did you know those areas were once part of the Persian Empire? It's fascinating, really, what stories those lands would tell if they could."

A few heads nodded before another passenger, a man in a navy blue cap, added, "Lands where empires rose and crumbled under the weight of war and revolution."

"That's right," Harvey said. "We'll pass over Turkey, too. Istanbul, the bridge between continents, a city that's seen its share in the clash of Christianity and Islam."

Melony blinked, the weight of Harvey's words shifting the mood. "I didn't know we'd see so much... conflict from above."

"It's not just conflict, though," Harvey said bluntly. "It's resilience. Stories of survival."

Madge and another attendant did a quick scan to see if their passengers were comfortable. With everything calm in the cabin, she asked, "It is definitely quite the journey, and it sounds like there is something bigger brewing between Edward and Mary, is that right?" She steered the conversation back to the story.

"Well," I continued, "his office did seem like it was a battlefield. One full of decisions and desires..."

* * *

"I love you." That's what he'd told her. That's what Mary heard. And for the next month, Mary was lost in a fog with Edward's declaration drifting around in her thoughts as a strange, uneasy feeling took root in the pit of her stomach. It wasn't until several days after she should have started her period that she realized she was late. Instinctively, there was no doubt she was with child but would have to wait several more weeks before confirming it.

After her appointment, she slipped into Edward's office, closing the door behind her. He looked up from his desk, already wanting her, until he saw something different in her eyes, something that concerned him. "Is something wrong?"

"I... I saw my doctor today," she said haltingly, tears rimming her dark blue eyes. "I'm pregnant."

Edward stood up behind his desk so abruptly that his leather executive chair smashed against the framed picture window behind his desk with a crash that resounded throughout the office.

"Good God," he snapped, slapping down the papers in his hand and then taking a deep breath. "It's nothing to get upset about, Mary. I'll pay for the abortion."

He stepped quickly around the desk, reaching to take her in his arms, he began to prattle, taking her limp hand in his and squeezing it, leading her toward the couch. "I wanted to talk with you about the plantation for the cocoa you have. I would like to go see it. I would like to see it with you, see if we can save the plants or maybe even the plantation."

Her knees buckled, plopping her to the couch. Looking up at his bending form, she said in a steady but quivering voice, "Mister Burke, I think we should talk about the baby before any discussion of a nonexistent plantation that I have nothing to do with."

For a penetrating instant, she stared at him, stared through him, straight past his handsome face and into his inner self, where he was crushingly calculating with cold precision. She observed the dimensions of this man. Arrogant bastard, she thought. The fog lifted. To him, her situation was straightforward, just another problem to be handled, an annoyance to be managed, an investment gone awry.

Of course, pregnancy was not what she wanted at this point in her life, but she wasn't going to have an abortion either. What am I going to do? She looked around the office, then snapped back to her immediate challenge: Edward the chocolate warrior, a title she'd coined in the doctor's office.

"Plain and simple, Mister Edward Burke, I'm not getting rid of the baby."

Squinting at her, he commanded, "You will damn well do what I say."

We'll see about that. "Edward," she beseeched him in an even calmer voice, "I understand that this isn't the best situation. God, how could it be for either of us? I know you're going through a tough time with Elizabeth, and I know I can't ask you to run away with me. . ." Slipping off the couch, stepping away from him, she continued, "But if you think for one second that I'm some sort of pushover, then you'll be in for another surprise, something much more burdensome than a helpless baby . . . and believe me, I am going to have this baby—no ifs, ands, or buts. And absolutely no abortion, Mister Burke!"

He sat with elbows on knees, and his chin cupped on top of clinched hands, indeed fists, as she stood over him, arms folded across her heaving chest.

"All right," he nodded. "Let me think of the best way for us to proceed. I'll come up with a plan . . ." His eyes held her stare. "One that will allow us both to move forward. For the time being, I ask that you don't say anything to anyone about the situation until we reach an amicable solution."

In the break room, Mary changed her shoes for more comfortable walkers and left early. She lived a couple of blocks south of the Mutual of Omaha Building in an apartment she'd furnished herself on the twelfth floor of Kensington Towers on 16th Street, right at the intersection with St. Mary's. Mary had grown up in a challenging environment, so this situation was not one that was going to knock her off her feet. As the oldest of six siblings in a military family, she was used to upheaval, moving from place to place due to her father's service in the US Air Force. The instability was compounded by her parents' strict and abusive parenting style; they believed that severe discipline was the only way to maintain order. Mary often pushed back,

87

tested the boundaries, tested to search for the love that she knew had to be there, somewhere.

When Mary was fourteen, her parents joined a religious cult in rural Nebraska. The group, led by a self-proclaimed prophet, promised spiritual enlightenment, communal living, and a path to salvation. At first, the community seemed close-knit, offering structure and purpose. But beneath the surface, its practices mirrored those of groups like Jim Jones's Peoples Temple—strict control, psychological manipulation, and a culture of fear disguised as faith.

Rules governed every aspect of daily life: clothing, speech, and even thoughts were subject to scrutiny. Questioning authority was seen as rebellion, punishable by public humiliation or isolation. Children, especially girls, bore the harshest treatment. They were expected to demonstrate unwavering obedience and endure physical and emotional discipline under the guise of spiritual purification. Education was limited, often replaced with indoctrination that reinforced the leader's teachings.

The group's doctrine twisted scripture into a tool of control. Members were taught that suffering brought them closer to God, a belief used to justify harsh punishments. Young girls were particularly vulnerable, groomed to serve the community's needs with little regard for their own well-being. The leader, like

Jim Jones, maintained power through intimidation, creating an environment where fear and loyalty became indistinguishable.

Mary, however, did not submit easily. Her defiance did not go unnoticed. The prophet, determined to break her spirit, made an example of her.

One winter evening, before the gathered congregation, Mary was dragged onto the raised wooden platform in the chapel. The air smelled of kerosene lamps and fear. Her wrists were bound, her thin dress offering little protection against the cold air seeping through the cracked wooden walls. The leader stood beside her, his voice echoing through the room as he condemned her defiance, warning others that rebellion led to damnation.

The punishment began without ceremony. A leather strap sliced through the air, striking her back with sharp, deliberate force. Each blow was meant to strip her of her will, to crush the spark of resistance within her. The congregation watched in silence—some with fear, others with hollow eyes that had long since learned to look away. Tears stung Mary's eyes, but she bit down on her cries, refusing to give them the satisfaction of her pain.

But the beatings were only the beginning. Over the following days, she was confined to a small, windowless room, deprived of food and sleep. The leaders called it purification—a way to cleanse her soul of defiance. Yet even as hunger gnawed at her stomach and exhaustion clouded her thoughts, the fire inside her refused to die. She whispered to herself in the dark, holding onto the belief that freedom existed beyond the compound's walls.

After weeks of planning and waiting for the right moment, Mary found her chance. One stormy night, while the wind howled against the buildings, she slipped through the shadows and into the woods beyond the compound's perimeter. The cold bit at her bare feet as she ran, branches scratching her arms and legs, but she did not stop. Hours later, soaked and trembling, she reached the nearest town and stumbled into the local sheriff's office.

The authorities listened to her story, but their hands were tied. The cult operated within the bounds of religious freedom, and without concrete evidence of criminal activity, there was little they could do. Mary's parents refused to speak against the group, leaving her with no home to return to. So the state placed her into foster care, severing her ties with the world she had escaped.

In her foster home, Mary encountered new challenges. Though her foster parents were not overtly harsh, the foster father's nighttime visits created an uneasy and uncomfortable situation. It wasn't violent, and he was kinder than anyone she had known, but he still violated the trust she was looking for in her life. Determined to break free from her circumstances, she had concentrated on finishing high school as quickly as possible, hoping education would provide her with a path forward.

Upon graduation, Mary moved to Omaha, looking to start anew. But she was on her own, with no reliable network or family to fall back on. Her parents were no longer an option, and her time in foster care had taught her to be wary.

When Mary first moved to Omaha, she took a job as a cocktail waitress at La Fiamma, a nightclub with velvet drapes, low amber lights, and an unspoken rule that what happened there stayed there. The clientele arrived in tailored suits, their shoes whispering on polished floors, and the air carried the faint scent of cigar smoke and power. The rumor that La Fiamma belonged to the mafia wasn't so much gossip as accepted truth, and Mary had learned quickly not to ask questions.

It was in the hum of that underworld, between balancing trays and dodging the watchful eyes of the other waitresses, that Benny noticed her. Benny, the boss's second son, had a presence that filled the quiet corners of the room like the low notes of a cello—impossible to ignore.

"Mary," he told her one night, his voice steady, deliberate, "you'll never have to work like the others. I'll make sure of it."

He wasn't boasting, and she believed him. Benny wasn't like the men who flung their wealth and influence around like confetti. He moved with the patience of someone who saw the long game. His eyes, dark and thoughtful, held the weight of a man who had spent his life observing and calculating, building solutions before problems had a chance to come to light.

Benny's kindness though was not weakness. To strangers, it might have seemed out of place when he stopped to carry an elderly neighbor's bags or bent down to tie the shoe of a child running past. But those gestures weren't empty—they reflected the code that Benny lived by, a quiet devotion to respect and protection. Children trusted him instinctively, wrapping their small hands around his as if they knew it was a safe harbor. His smile, warm and patient, had none of the sharpness that edged Edward Burke's grin.

But he wasn't soft either. If you crossed him—if you betrayed him or harmed those under his care—his vengeance was a slow tide, inevitable and crushing. He never acted in haste, his decisions steeped in thought and precision. His methods weren't brutish; they were surgical, exacting. To Benny, conflict was a failure only if it ended without a lesson learned.

For Mary, Benny was an enigma. She'd seen his brilliance in motion, the way his mind worked like a chessboard in perpetual motion, every piece exactly where it needed to be. And though she was rough around the edges, untamed in ways she couldn't always control, Benny saw potential in her. He didn't want a decoration or a fleeting affair; he wanted a partner. He liked her fire, but he also wanted to shape it into something that fit his world.

When Mary explained she wasn't ready for such a commitment, he let her go, firing her for both their sakes. He gave her a small severance so she could get out of that world of nightclubs, a place Benny said she didn't belong to. Part of her severance was a small satchel of cocoa beans along with their story. So, with his encouragement, she began looking at other career possibilities outside of the smoke-filled rooms of the night. And that is how she met Edward, a man who saw her potential one night while she was waiting tables and offered her a position as his private secretary. Even after starting to work for Edward, Mary had continued to see Benny off and on.

When she first found out about her pregnancy, she had reluctantly withheld the information from both Benny and Edward. Ultimately, she decided she could only tell Edward because Benny would want to get married and start a family. She didn't want to add to the complication of the situation by marrying someone she did not love. Plus, he would not have been so happy to hear she had been with Edward, too, and decided never to speak to Benny again. But now, she wondered, what kind of future could she offer a child? Pregnancy had been the last thing she expected. She'd taken precautions, using a diaphragm. Oh, how could I be so stupid? she thought.

That evening the doorbell rang with a messenger holding a large brown envelope for which she had to sign. She sat herself at her kitchen dinette, poured a glass of Merlot, and opened the envelope. The long legal document rambled on for twelve pages. She laughed at some of the language Edward's attorney Jim, a bespectacled double for a young Cary Grant, had concocted. But she had to give him credit, after all, for how often the straitlaced Jim wrote agreements between knocked-up administrative assistants and executives worth tens of millions of dollars. Well, she told herself, maybe it's not that rare, people being people.

The next morning, with the document locked under her arm in the messenger envelope, Mary walked purposely toward Edward's office. She wore her black wrapped skirt and black tights along with a revealing, white chiffon blouse she'd picked out days before for just for this moment.

"Why, don't you look lovely today," said Edward as she entered his office. "Please have a seat." He motioned toward the couch. Mary ignored his direction and plopped down in a cushioned, maroon leather wingback chair near the corner of his desk, one where clients and businesspeople sat. She feigned a bright smile at the man before her. He wore a blue shirt with an Oxford collar, a blue silk tie, and what she assumed was a thousand-dollar Italian suit, dusty grey with subtle tan pinstripes. He leaned back in his black leather chair, locked his fingers behind his neck, elbows raised like wings about to flap, and spoke in his skilled, relaxed style. "What did you think of the contract?"

"Well, it's generous, but of course, I have some questions," Mary said.

"Shoot."

"First of all," she began, having memorized her lines, rehearsing them since her alarm clock sang that morning. "Mister Burke, why can't I stay in my own apartment? I don't want to leave."

"You don't need to stay where you are. In fact, you'll be better off leaving," he assured her. "You and the baby will both receive first-rate medical care where you are going; all your needs will be met."

"They could just as easily be met at my apartment; it's my home." Her fingers traced along the intricately stitched seam running down the leather armrest of the chair.

"Do you want this baby, Mary?" he asked flatly.

"Yes." She folded her hands in front of her.

"Then you will stay with my friends. You will call your parents; tell them you are helping a woman with a difficult pregnancy as a kind of personal assistant."

"That makes no sense. Why can't I tell my parents that it's my baby?" she asked with the commanding voice of an interrogator, then added in her mind, not that I talk to them much anyway.

He thought for a moment, regrouping. He leaned slightly toward her, then slapped the desk with his palms. "You know, Mary, I am letting you have this child. I trust you to uphold your end of the deal; you know full well I cannot afford the potential repercussions of this pregnancy. You damn well will leave town, and you will do exactly what I tell you to do. Do you understand? It's all in the contract."

Mary blinked as her rehearsed determination dissolved under the withering fire of a skilled forty-five-year-old financial wizard who now flaunted his masculine aura in ways that had nothing to do with attracting females with charm; she saw before her a masculine tyrant, a dictator, a caricature of that jerk in The Tempest. What was his name? her brain flipped through Shakespeare's play, desperate for escape. That's it, Prospero. Only with Edward, the jerk became Prosperous; all he could think or feel was financial tactics. I'm surprised he can father something other than a dollar; well, maybe he didn't.

She blinked again, dousing welling tears, and nodded acquiescently to his demands.

"You will stay with Eleanor and Bud. You will have everything you and the baby need, and you will not tell anyone this is my child, absolutely no one. Is that clear?"

She nodded again.

"If anyone asks, you'll say that the father is away. Did you find the ring in the envelope?" He reached for a folder on his desk that she supposed contained a copy of the agreement. It did.

"The little gold band?"

He nodded.

"Yes, I saw it."

"Wear it. That way if you do go out, no one will think twice about your pregnancy."

He brandished the blue-jacketed agreement. "You will sign this document which states the same. You will continue to get your pay, plus a little bonus."

"A bonus? What for?" Mary asked.

Edward leaned toward her, handing her the agreement. "Look, you sign, I explain, okay?"

"Sure, Mister Burke, but what's the bonus for?"

"It's to pay you for some work at the farm where you'll be with Bud and Eleanor. I want you to help with a little investment I've made; it's a subject you know something about."

"What investment is that?"

"It's chocolate, Mary," he said, a know-it-all arrogance in his tone. "I thought this would be fun for you. I had been planning to surprise you with this before you became with, you know, that." He pointed at her midline.

Mary exploded. "That? That is a child!"

"Sign the damned agreement, woman."

Mary scribbled her signature and tossed the document across the desk. "There," she mumbled angrily, "you can mail me my copy when you've signed it, too. I'll be at Bud's."

She rose, patting her black wrap skirt, then stood facing Edward like a soldier at attention. "That was a stupid investment, by the way. I know nothing about chocolate, and from this day forward, I hate it!"

"Don't say you hate it, Mary; that is just childish. You need to grow up now." His condescending words made her insides boil. "I bought a little confectionary company. I thought you'd enjoy making changes, improving it, adding your special touch, and of course, somewhere down the line, after the front end is intelligently designed, we could integrate backward into raw materials, into that plantation, wherever it is."

"I do not know much about confectionaries, Mister Burke. To tell the truth, this whole situation is overwhelming to me right now. I feel like I am getting steamrolled. I don't like it. I don't trust any of this . . ." She pointed to the agreement on his desk and tossed her messenger envelope on top of it. Then she collapsed again into the maroon chair with a resounding plop!

Edward immediately rose and strode to stand over her, he placed a hand gently on her shoulder, feeling the chiffon blouse crinkle under his touch. She shivered.

"Mary, there is nothing to be overwhelmed by. There is nothing not to trust. We will talk about it after you are settled with Bud and Eleanor. If you are not comfortable there, we can make other arrangements. Give them a chance, though. They are kind and will take care of you. You can read over our agreement papers again if you want. Sit here and take your time."

"I know what they say, Mister Burke," she said in a monotone voice, determined to maintain her dignity. "It is essentially a business agreement that deals with the fundamentals of a new life and keeps the creators of that new life at arm's length, keeping our secret from the civilized world."

"Yes, it says you will keep the pregnancy private," he continued in his condescending tone. "You are being paid for agreeing to that."

"Honestly, Edward, if I'm supposed to be helping a pregnant woman, won't it look strange when I am the one who gets big and round? My parents certainly will not buy the story at that point."

"Mary, your parents won't be visiting you. I know about your family."

"Okay, so they won't visit, but they're eventually going to find out that I have a baby. What about my friends? I can't just go missing for seven or eight months. Have you actually thought about all this? Because it seems to me, it's a little strange."

"We have that covered. Surely you read the logic in the agreement. Your friends will understand you have an exciting new job, which pays better. It's only a few months, Mary. Your friends will be fine; you'll be fine."

"All this just because you want to know where the plantation is located. I know that is what you want, but what if I cannot give it to you? It really is my friend's story, not mine."

Her comments left him with a newly sprouting seed of doubt.

"Now look, there will be plenty of . . . time to talk about where the plantation is located—" He looked into her eyes, only to be interrupted.

"Sorry, old boy," she said, rising. "It's a family secret, one that doesn't belong to me."

* * *

Spontaneous applause echoed through our part of the cabin. Apparently, the storytelling had got a bit animated, my voice quietly rising in excitement with Mary's determination and attracting a much wider audience than Damion, Harvey, and Melony.

While passing out small bottles of water, Madge said, "That poor girl and her randy boss. I'd boil him in chocolate, I would."

Melony shifted in her seat, her eyes thoughtful. "What about Mary's family? Did her siblings ever leave the cult? What about her parents? Did they ever find each other again?"

"Yes," I replied. "Her siblings all left the cult, one by one, as they grew older. Even her parents eventually found the strength to leave. It didn't happen overnight—healing from something like that takes time. Years passed before they truly found their way back to each other, but when they did, something remarkable happened."

I paused, picturing the invisible threads that bound them together. "They became closer than they'd ever been. Maybe it was the shared experience—the unspoken understanding of what they'd survived. They rarely spoke about the abuse, but they didn't need to. They were survivors—but more than that, they became people who cherished life with an unmatched gratitude. Every laugh, every celebration, every ordinary day—they embraced it all because they knew the value of freedom and joy. It's part of what made Mary, even after everything, carry strength with her."

Chapter Seven

Sixty miles west of Omaha, a white farmhouse kept its counsel behind a wall of red cedar—the state's model windbreak, grown into a quiet barricade. Beds where tomatoes and rhubarb had run riot in summer now lay under a neat pelt of leaves.

A cold storm brewed above, tumbling into the pages of the Tempest as Mary sat rubbing her swollen belly beneath the giant sycamore tree. "Ariel," she said. Ariel, who was a captive servant to Prospero, reminds her master that he promised her freedom a year early if she performed certain tasks. "How prophetic," Mary ran her finger across the name, "that one day you shall be free from Prospero too."

If the sycamore had ears instead of leaves — which had all fallen earlier that fall — it might have heard Mary whisper to the child within, "How am I going to take care of you? Was Edward right?"

A sharp rustle came from behind. For an instant she thought the trees had answered — or warned her. Then the man himself stepped through. Mary stared straight ahead, avoiding eye contact.

"How's it going?" he asked, pulling up a wicker chair; a small table stood between them, and a glass of hot cider sitting on it twittered a bit, sloshing when the arm of Edward's chair bumped it. He wore a brown woolen suit, looking more a country gentleman than someone who lived in the city.

I bet he bought that suit just for this visit, she thought while saying, "Everything's fine."

"I'm glad." He reached to pat her knee, which she moved away.

"There's one exception to feeling fine, though, Edward. Eleanor told me the baby was up for adoption. I do not recall having that discussion."

"You can keep the damn baby. All I want from you is help with the chocolate," he said, trying to suppress the frustration that was brewing inside with this woman he had gone out of his way to help. But he kept himself in check. He was good at acting like the boy next door when needed.

"Is that in the contract?" she asked through the hidden tension between them.

"That's why I'm here. We need to reach a verbal agreement about the baby and the chocolate; then I'll have Jim write out what we decide and bring the contract out for you to sign himself."

He lifted the glass of cider from the weathered garden table, offering it to her.

She shook her head. "No, thank you."

Edward drained the glass in several loud gulps.

"I think we should start talking about your role in the confectionary business. Overall, the business has good products, and we are looking at expanding the market for them. Taking them into other states."

"Yes, I know. Bud brought me some chocolate caramels and lollipops. They're really good."

"I want you involved," he said with an authoritative tone.

Mary raised her eyebrows. "You keep saying that. I've heard your words. But you need to listen to mine. I told you, I do not know anything about candy."

"That's not entirely true now, is it? I would like to know more about your family's cocoa. We can save it," Edward's voice softened, "You and I can share it with the world." He took out a map and several papers from a folder he had brought.

"You mean monetize it. Bring it to everyone, because who are we to withhold such a luxury?" The late afternoon sun stretched its amber fingers over the rolling hills, casting long shadows across the farmhouse yard. The air was heavy with the earthy scent of drying hay. Mary sat with one hand resting protectively on the small swell of her stomach, her eyes steady as she faced Edward.

"I've told you everything I know, Edward," she said, her voice soft but unwavering. "The cocoa didn't come from my family. It was just a story I heard, nothing more."

Edward's jaw clenched, the lines of exhaustion deepening across his face. "A story?" He let out a bitter laugh, sharp and hollow. "After what I experienced, and after all this time, you expect me to believe that this"—he gestured wildly to the crumbling notes, maps, and failed leads that seemed to haunt him—"was all for a story?"

"It was a tale told to me, passed like whispers in the dark," Mary said. A cold breeze rustled the last of the dead leaves still clinging to the oaks, punctuating the quiet strength in her tone. "I never said it belonged to my family. You've twisted it into something it isn't."

Edward's eyes narrowed, searching her face for a crack in her calm exterior, something to cling to. "Then tell me who it was," he demanded, his voice tight with desperation. "Who gave you the cocoa, if not your family?"

A shadow of sadness crossed Mary's features. She took a deep breath and looked out over the fields, their golden hue catching the last rays of sunlight. "Edward," she said, turning back to him, "you need to understand—I won't say any more. There are some things that should stay where they belong."

His frustration flared into anger, a sudden storm threatening to break. "Do you know what this means to me?" His fist tightened, "Mary, do you understand?" The plea in his voice was unmistakable, the echo of all the nights spent chasing ghosts.

"I know," Mary whispered. "More than anyone, I know. But this isn't something I can help you with. Please . . . let it go."

But Edward's gaze was already somewhere far beyond the rolling fields, searching for answers he refused to believe weren't there. The bare branches whispered overhead, carrying Mary's silent hope that he would one day hear her words and finally listen. "Well, you've got a choice to make. I'm not coming back out here. I'm sending Jim Backlish with two contracts; this will be in your hands."

After Edward stormed off, Mary tried to contemplate what he would be up to next. She settled in with the knowledge that the secret cocoa had prevailed, at least momentarily, over the mighty Edward Burke. "Why won't he listen? It was just a story that was taken too far," she said with an audible humph.

***

The quiet of Jack Robert's study was interrupted by the jangle of the phone, its ring slicing through the room's rich mahogany stillness. He reached for it, half-expecting another routine client call, but the clipped voice that came through set his senses on edge.

"Jack, it's Edward Burke."

"Edward, good to hear from you. What can I help you with?" Jack leaned back in his chair, eyes fixed on the overhead lamp.

"A matter that requires, discretion," Edward replied. "It concerns a young woman named Mary. She's employed under certain arrangements of mine and is now with child. It's . . . complicated."

Jack sat up to focus on the conversation. He knew enough about Edward to understand that "complicated" often came with unseen strings. "Go on."

"This child, Jack—Mary's intent on keeping it, but she's alone, with no means to speak of. It won't be long before her circumstances force a change of heart. When that time comes, I want the path already set."

Jack felt the shift, the click of Edward's strategy unfolding like a well-oiled mechanism. "You're talking adoption?"

"Yes, I am. And I thought of your daughter Emily. She and William have been looking to grow their family, have they not?

This is an opportunity to solve many problems at once, in a way that benefits everyone involved. But only if handled delicately."

Jack's face tightened, memories of William's quiet frustration and Emily's wistful glances at other mothers surfacing in his mind. "You know they've been hoping for another child, Edward. But this... Does Mary know what you're planning?"

"Not yet. She's clinging to the promise of better days, but reality has a way of revising those hopes. And when it does, I need someone who understands discretion, who can make sure this remains a closed circle. That's where you come in."

Jack processed Edward's words. The appeal wasn't just in the adoption itself, but in the trust Edward placed in him. A matter of mutual interests and understanding the stakes—a child woven into a web that touched on Edward's deep, enigmatic ventures.

"You know I won't break confidence," Jack said at last. "But this is a significant step."

"I wouldn't ask otherwise. When the time comes, it'll be your word that reassures William and Emily. All I need now is your consideration, Jack." Edward's voice lowered, settling the matter with the gravity of an oath unspoken but known.

"You'll have it," Jack said, the finality in his own voice confirming his commitment and the shift in their intertwined fates.

"Good," Edward responded, his relief as subtle as a whispered sigh. The call ended, leaving Jack in the quiet room, now thick with the weight of what was to come.

* * *

Within a week of the phone call, Bud and Eleanor ushered Edward's attorney Jim, with eyeglasses larger than Olympic rings, before Mary in the lazy yard, where she sat wrapped in a thick wool blanket.

"Want me to stay?" asked Eleanor. "I can. Bud's got to check the animals."

"No, that's all right. I know Jim here. Hello, Jim."

Jim Backlish sat in the wicker chair and placed his papers on the little garden table.

* * *

"I don't really want to interrupt," said Melony. "But this farmer Bud guy; is he a spy? I mean Edward's obviously paying them, isn't he? And what about this Jack. How are he and Edward connected?"

"I don't have the exact details on what transpired between Bud and Edward, or Jack and Edward—I wasn't there. But I can tell you what I do know—Oh!" The plane dropped and tilted suddenly.

Damion touched my shoulder to interrupt. "The plane just tilted to the right as it modified course Don't worry, we are probably turning to avoid some weather. It's amazing that all we hear is a faint dull hum, because at this altitude we are cruising at Mach 0.85. That's about 652 miles per hour. We've left the engine noise behind," Damion explained upon seeing one of the passengers show a little anxiety.

"I say," said Harvey, "you are broadly educated, aren't you?"

"Oh, not really, just like technical stuff, but before I got my master's in business what I really studied were languages."

"Languages, eh?" said Harvey. "You can help me. I've never understood why the Australian Labor Party used the American spelling."

"That's more history than language, Harvey," said Damion. "The party was founded as a federal party prior to the first sitting of the Australian Parliament in 1901 but is descended from labor parties in various Australian colonies, formally beginning a decade earlier in 1891. The spelling was a compromise."

"Compromise, eh?"

"So, was Mary compromised by Bud and Eleanor?" asked Melony. "I mean, I guess you'd have to guess that, wouldn't you?"

"No, years later when I was researching this story, I came across Eleanor's journal. She and Bud weren't so much friends of Edward Burke as they were indebted to him. Farm prices had collapsed in one of those cyclical economic downturns. Bud leveraged 600 acres to double them and ended up out of his depth financially. That's when Edward helped bail him out." The plane bounced again. "In regard to Edward and Jack, in 1967, a quiet deal was struck—one that would ripple across decades and change the financial world forever. Jack sold his cherished creation, National Insurance Company, to Edward. The price? $8 million. The true value? Immeasurable."

National Insurance wasn't just another insurance firm; it was created in 1940 from Jack's belief that risk could be tamed with the right assessment. He famously said, "There are no bad risks, only bad prices," an adage that guided his company's unconventional approach. While other insurers turned away from peculiar challenges, National Insurance leaned in, offering coverage to those deemed uninsurable.

Edward, ever the seeker of value, recognized not only the profitability of Jack's business model but also the brilliance of the man behind it. After careful evaluation, Edward offered Jack $35 per share. Jack countered with $50 and shares in Edward's company, a bold demand that could have ended negotiations. But Burke, known for his keen eye for long-term gains, saw there was still untold value to be had in Jack's number. A handshake sealed the deal.

That moment was more than a transaction; it was the spark that ignited a transformation. For Edward, the acquisition of National Insurance was a gateway into the insurance industry—a sector whose steady cash flows would become the bedrock of his empire.

It's a story of foresight, daring, and the power of calculated risks—a reminder that sometimes, the greatest treasures lie hidden in the unconventional.

"In that case, was Burke also a man who played chess?" asked Harvey. "I mean, it seems that way to me."

"Please continue." Damion's stomach growled. "We've got time before they start dinner service. Could you talk a bit about Benny and his family? It is their cocoa, after all. That is what Mary was trying to say, right?"

My mind flipped to Benny's family like fanning pages in a book. "The D'Angelo family, Benny's lineage, had long held a reputation shrouded in whispers and nods around the smoky back rooms of Omaha's nightclubs. They weren't just known for their lucrative bookmaking operations or the velvet-lined gambling halls that thrived during Prohibition and well into mid-century; no, their legacy ran deeper, tangled with a tale few dared to recall out loud. It was said that long before Tom Dennison's empire turned Omaha into a hotbed of vice, the D'Angelos had found themselves entrusted with something far more potent than the finest scotch or bootleg liquor—the legendary cocoa.

"Benny's several-greats-grandfather, Antonio D'Angelo, was an immigrant shoe repairman who knew no power beyond his hammer and awl, and stumbled into the world of the cocoa trade through the most unlikely of means. The story, passed down through hushed kitchen table confessions, spoke of a night in a Sicilian port where Antonio had saved a merchant's life from a trio of cutthroat smugglers."

* * *

1888

The air in the Sicilian port was thick with the brine of the sea and the faint scent of tar, the narrow streets winding like veins through the city, pulsing with life even under the cloak of night. Antonio D'Angelo, a shoemaker, walked home from his workshop, the echo of his steady footsteps drowned out by the raucous laughter spilling from the taverns. He was a man who knew power only in the precise strike of his hammer, the resilience of worn leather under his awl. But tonight, fate would set him on a path far beyond his simple trade.

He turned down a shadowed alley, one he took each night without thought, but tonight it was different. The sounds of struggle, muted and sharp, came from deeper within. Antonio's instincts tightened in his chest. He should have kept walking, head down, like any man who understood the unspoken rules of the port. But a cry, desperate and final, cut through the darkness.

Against his better judgment, Antonio stepped closer, eyes adjusting to the dim glow of a hanging lantern. Three figures loomed over a fourth, the glint of blades catching the flicker of the flame. The man on the ground, draped in silken robes foreign to this rough town, clutched a small satchel to his chest.

"Leave him." Antonio's voice was steadier than he felt, the words an instinct more than a decision. The thugs turned, their faces twisted with surprise that quickly morphed into something cruel. The leader, a scarred man with eyes as flat and cold as a sword's edge, stepped forward, testing Antonio's resolve.

"A hero tonight, eh?" the scarred man sneered, his voice thick with derision and the cold promise of violence. The glint of the blade in his hand caught the lantern light, a cruel smile wrought in steel.

Antonio's muscles tensed, his heartbeat thundering in his ears. There was no time to question his impulse; survival demanded he move or perish. The first attacker struck with a speed that would have gutted a lesser man, the knife whistling through the narrow space where Antonio's neck had been just moments before. He twisted to the side, the scent of salt and rust filling his nose as the blade barely grazed his collar. Without pause, Antonio drove his shoulder into the man's ribs, the force sending him stumbling back, the grunt of pain escaping him like air from

The second attacker advanced with a snarl, dark eyes flashing under a mop of greasy hair. Antonio felt the scrape of the cobblestones under his boots as he braced himself, raising his forearm just in time to deflect a wild swing. The impact numbed his arm, but a burst of strength kicked in before the pain could settle. He lashed out with a sharp elbow, connecting squarely with the man's jaw. A sickening crack echoed down the alley, and the attacker's eyes rolled back as he crumpled to the ground like a rag doll, the knife clattering uselessly from his hand.

Antonio's ragged breaths and the still-shivering merchant huddled against the wall. The third man stood frozen, his confidence shattered as he stared at his fallen comrades. He glanced between Antonio, who stood with his chest heaving, and the merchant, who clutched the satchel to his chest. The man's resolve cracked, and fear overtook whatever loyalty or greed had held him in place. His retreat was quick and clumsy, boots grating on stone as he disappeared into the night, a rat abandoning a burning ship.

Antonio's vision pulsed with the adrenaline coursing through his veins. The metallic taste of blood lingered on his tongue, and he could feel the shallow cut on his forearm stinging in the cool sea air. He wiped the sweat from his brow, eyes flicking to the merchant who slowly pushed himself upright, his eyes wide and dark, reflecting the wavering lantern light.

"Grazie, signore," the man whispered. He shifted, and the rich fabric of his robe rustled, the sound oddly soft after the chaos that had just unfolded. With a shaky breath, he stepped forward, hands trembling as he held out the small satchel that had nearly cost him his life.

Antonio blinked, confusion knitting his brow as he looked at the man, then at the offered bundle. "I don't—" he started, but the merchant cut him off with a fierce urgency.

"You saved more than a life tonight," he said, his eyes locking onto Antonio's with a gravity that made the shoemaker's pulse quicken for an entirely different reason. "Guard these as you would your own life."

Before Antonio could ask what was inside, the merchant pressed the satchel into his hands and turned, his silhouette swallowed by the shadows before Antonio could protest.

He looked down at the satchel in his hands, its edges frayed but sturdy, and felt the first shiver of destiny trace down his spine. He stood motionless, the sounds of the port gradually returning, the shouts of fishermen, the creak of ships—and with it, a sense of unreality. His hands trembled as he opened the satchel. The scent hit him first, deep and earthy, with a subtle, almost floral sweetness. Inside were dark beans, more lustrous than any he'd seen, their crackled surface catching the dim light like polished onyx.

The whispers began that night, the story of how Antonio D'Angelo, the shoemaker, came to possess a secret so potent it would twist the fate of his family for generations. The beans were revered, hidden behind wooden panels in the workshop, spoken of only in the quiet of candle-lit kitchens when trust was absolute. It was said they came from the deep jungle where shamans guarded them with rites older than memory, a cocoa that could awaken the mind and sharpen the senses.

Years later, when Antonio's life ebbed away under the weight of age, he called for his son to kneel beside him. The small satchel was placed in the boy's hands.

"Guard these, as I did," Antonio whispered, eyes glassy with the weight of the promise. "They are more than they seem, and so too are we."

The son, a young man, wide-eyed, nodded, the scent of the cocoa forever etching itself into the marrow of his bones. The night air outside the window stirred, carrying with it the legacy that would follow the D'Angelos from the shadowed ports of Sicily to the hidden rooms of Omaha, where deals were whispered and lives were gambled away.

* * *

"By the time Benny was born in 1947, the cocoa was a story his father half-remembered, a relic buried under decades of racketeering, bootleg deals, and alliances with names like Frank Calamia and the enigmatic Anthony Biase.

"As Benny rose in power, turning the D'Angelo syndicate into one of the largest bookmaking operations in the Midwest, he continued to hear fragmented stories about the cocoa. He learned that Antonio's mysterious merchant might have been more than a simple tradesman, that the cocoa had spiritual and intoxicating properties known only to a few, and that some believed it held the power to alter the fate of those who consumed it. The secret of its origin was said to be safeguarded somewhere in the South American rainforests, known only by alchemists and ancient tribes who treated the beans as sacred.

"But in their rapid shift from cocoa guardians to kingpins of racketeering and bootlegging, the D'Angelo family had lost their connection to the secret. Benny's focus shifted to protecting his family's empire in a city where organized crime wore a suit and sat at the same table as the lawyers."

"And so, this is the legacy Benny handed to Mary?" Harvey's words questioned Benny's choice.

"He did," I said. "And even if she did not know exactly what she held, she didn't want to put them in the wrong hands either."

***

"I think we've got some good agreements here," young Backlish said.

I bet you do. You wrote them, Mary thought, suspicious of any man who wore Old Spice aftershave. It reminded her of Edward.

Bud left to tend to the farm before any hot tempers arose.

Eleanor smoothed her gingham apron and took a step toward the house. "I'll fetch some coffee for you. And the usual for you, Mary?"

"Thank you." Her face flushed with a quickening in the pit of her stomach.

"You feeling all right?" Eleanor asked before heading to the house.

"Yeah, I'm fine."

"Will that be your fancy chocolate?" Jim asked.

"I don't know how fancy it will be, but if you are talking about what Edward is so keen on, no. It is just whatever chocolate Eleanor uses. And here I thought you came to wish me a merry winter solstice," Mary answered.

Ignoring the sarcasm, Jim Backlish leaned forward over the documents on the. "How much do you have left? The chocolate?

I promise not to tell."

Mary leaned in too. "Okay," she whispered, "but remember, you just promised not to tell."

Backlish's tongue swiped over his lips; he swallowed and focused on her with an intent stare.

"I don't have much; a handful is all that remains," you toad, "But Jim, it's just a game. Edward's imagination has got the best of him, and he won't let it go."

"And the cocoa beans, can you tell me where they really are? Where they grow? Or better yet, can you tell me who gave them to you?" Jim asked.

Mary sighed, then closing her eyes for a moment, said, "If you want my opinion on this what Edward is looking for, it is long gone, if it ever existed at all. It was a fable. And if it really did exist, it probably died with the tale." Mary's face scrunched with an uncomfortable ache.

Jim sat back, watching her rearrange in her seat. "Are you okay?" he asked warily.

"I'm fine." She readjusted her position. "Just a little ache in my back." Then feeling nauseous, she said, "Actually, I'm not feeling so well. Can we go inside?"

"Are you, I mean . . ." Jim looked at her. "Do you think you are in labor?"

"I am two weeks away. It's probably all the cold air and stress about Edward and the chocolate and things I do not know. Why? Are you afraid you will have to help deliver a baby instead of the papers?"

"Well, no. But, if it were delivery time, Mary, we'd certainly have to get these papers signed without delay. So, let's do that. Let's get these signed so we can take it off your list of worries."

"You're all business, aren't you?" Mary said, reaching for the folder.

"Not really," he said, smiling with sudden brightness. "Mary, I know this is a difficult decision for you, but I'm here to help."

"Difficult decision? What are you talking about?" Mary shook her head in confusion.

"You know, I had a crush on you when I first came to the office . . ." Jim began droning on and on about something.

Who needs this? she thought, and his voice drifted into the blue sky where it got swallowed up by some passing clouds, leaving only a sense of tranquility. The tranquility, however, only lasted a moment, because as soon as Eleanor returned to the yard with a tray, wham!

"Oooooh!" Mary doubled over, gripping her chair. What was that? Should I start counting the minutes until the next pain comes?

Standing quickly, Jim spat out, "I knew it. I just knew it." He looked at Mary. "I told you something was wrong."

"Nothing is wrong," said Eleanor. "But you better gather up them papers, Mister Lawyer. You are about to make one hairy-assed flying trip to the hospital 'cause I don't see Bud anywhere and we've got an hour's drive ahead of us."

They walked beside Mary while she waddled slowly out of the lazy yard, leaving behind the small garden table, mugs of coffee, a half-glass of chocolate, two empty chairs, and a squirrel jumping between dormant branches. In front of them, the white farmhouse and Jim Backlish's black Jaguar. She winced at the next contraction. It was so much milder than that first doozy, she thought, maybe false alarm?

It wasn't.

Chapter Eight

"I can smell our dinner heating up, thank goodness," Damion said as his stomach growled, obviously needing attention. "I think Madge said something about steak."

He was right; we were brought trays with steaks measuring two by three inches, a baked potato, a small salad, and a cheesecake with strawberry sauce.

"Shall we take a break while we eat or..."

"Keep going," a few food-stuffed voices echoed. "If you don't mind."

* * *

Eleanor held Mary's knotted hands in the tan leather rear seat of the speeding black Jaguar while Jim drove with his head bent forward at what felt like 100 miles an hour. Eleanor felt sure he had visions of Le Mans cruising through his lawyerly head; he probably saw himself as Steve McQueen.

While the ride may have only been fifty-two minutes long, for Mary that didn't matter; the only time that existed was the time between contractions. Which remained safely distanced until the car came to a screeching halt at Creighton University Hospital in Omaha.

"Not bad driving, Mister Backlish," Eleanor said, opening the door and helping Mary inside.

In the hospital, uniformed nurses and orderlies systematically went about their duties. They helped dress Mary in a gown and get into bed. It all seemed surreal and a little oddly routine to Mary. It felt more like her body took over, and she was along as a spectator even though the pain sought to remind her that she was an active participant.

Wham! "Ouch! Oh God, that hurts!" Mary grimaced. The series of contractions began morphing into one long, intense span of pain and an urge to push. She pleaded, "Ohhhh, help me!"

"Push!" the doctor urged.

Bright light from the silver hanging lamp temporarily blinded Mary before her eyelids tightened together, squeezing shut. The knuckles on her hands went white as she gripped the low metal handrails on the bed. Sweat beaded her brow. She could barely take another breath when the doctor instructed her again, "Push, Mary. You're almost there."

Exhausted and unable to feel any strength, her body somehow surged with the deepest and longest contraction. "This is it, Mary, this is it. Just a little more..."

The doctor looked up, releasing a bit of his own adrenaline to announce, "It's a girl!" Mary heard Ariel's glorious cry, the first sound of her newborn daughter. Smiling, she lifted her arms, asking the nurse to bring the baby to her.

Instead, she was injected with a sedative. "Eleanor," she cried, "tell them I want my baby." Her eyes softened with her sinking spirit as she drew in a deep breath. After that, everything went blank.

* * *

Mary drifted in a haze, the world around her dissolving into fragments of thought and sensation. Time folded in on itself, blurring moments into a dream of sunlit grass and the familiar comfort of the lazy yard. She could feel Eleanor's presence beside her, as steady as the rhythm of their afternoons together. But then, the dream shifted. Eleanor slipped away, heading toward the house, surely to fetch her usual tea.

"Eleanor?" The word fragile on her cracked lips. A rush of air moved in with the opening door, pulling her upward from the fog. For a moment, she clung to the hope that it was Eleanor returning. "Is that you?"

The response was a man's voice, faintly familiar yet laced with a weight that settled heavy in the air. "Eleanor won't be coming back." wheels scratched against the floor as he swung the stool into place beside her bed. "How do you feel?"

Her eyelids struggled against the thickness holding them shut. The scent came next—cloying, sharp, and distinctly male. It hovered in the dryness of her nose and throat, refusing to disperse. Her mind fumbled for recognition, grasping at the scent that clung so stubbornly to the sterile room.

Then it hit her: Old Spice.

Jim Backlish all but knelt at her side, having purloined the obstetrician's wheeled, low-seated stool so he could scoot close. She sensed they were alone. Her eyebrows lifted, trying to heave the weight of her lids up.

"Where is my baby? Where is Eleanor?" she mumbled to Jim, agitated, suddenly irritable. "Where the fuck is Eleanor?" Sitting up and taking in her surroundings, fogged by the after-effects of morphine, the first observation she had was thinking, what a very sterile room. It took a few more long, forced blinks before she could open her eyes fully, looking squarely at Jim, and upon seeing those large-rimmed spectacles, she decided it was better to be asleep and retreated back to her pillow.

"We don't have much time for these games, Mary," Jim said. "I know you are awake."

"I have all the time in the world," she answered defiantly. "Can you tell them to please bring my baby. I have to nurse her. Getting started right is important, you know."

"Mary, do you mind sitting back up? I'd like to talk with you for a minute."

Mary shuffled, scooted into a sitting position, and rubbed her eyes. "What do you want to talk about? Is my daughter okay? Can I see her?"

Jim placed his hand over the breast pocket of his dark blue suit. His tie was a dull grey. It matches his personality, she thought. He took a deep breath, as though preparing to launch a board room presentation, and said simply, "That's why I am here."

"What's why you're here?"

"I will be helping you through the adoption."

"What adoption? What are you talking about?" Now Mary was sitting up completely. The lingering effects of the drugs wore off instantly.

"I'm Jim Backlish, remember? I brought the Edward Burke contracts to the farm. Then I drove you here with Eleanor. Do you remember?"

"Oh, come on. I know who you are." Her voice was annoyed. "But I do not remember anything about an adoption!"

"Mary, my job is to help you. Okay? No need to raise your voice at me." Jim spoke as he would a child.

"I didn't sign any contracts, did I, Jim?" Mary asked while thinking back to the farmhouse, scanning her memory for any papers she might've signed. But Jim hadn't been at the house that long before she'd gone into labor, and she was sure she hadn't signed anything.

"Try to follow me here, Mary." He paused, looking at her. "Is your mouth dry? The nurse has left a pitcher of water. Shall I pour some for you?" He decanted water from an aluminum pitcher and handed Mary the paper cup. "Here, sip this; there are ice chips in it. Now, try to follow what I am saying, okay?"

"Okay," she said cautiously. "Thank you for the water." She was momentarily soothed by the ice chips, allowing them to melt against the inside of her cheek.

Starting over, clearing his throat, Jim launched into his well-rehearsed speech. "Mary, I am here to help you through the adoption of your daughter. She will be in the hands of a very nice couple. A couple that can give her a stable and loving home. She will be part of a family, a stable, loving family."

In a grindingly steady, clear voice, Mary said, "I did not give my baby up for adoption."

Jim jumped in before she had the chance to continue. "Before you go off your hinges, please listen to me." He raised his hands in a truce. "You don't have to go through with the adoption. You have two choices." He moved the heavy frame of his glasses back up the bridge of his nose. "Here's the deal. I have two contracts."

Mary interrupted, "I already signed the contract. I told him I wouldn't tell anyone, and I didn't." She fought stubbornly to hold back tears.

"That was just a confidentiality agreement. We've moved beyond that. Now you will choose between two contracts. You can walk away free with this check for $10,000 in exchange for your troubles. This will give you a fresh start after the adoption." He waved the check.

"Jim, you aren't listening," she sobbed. "There will be no adoption. That's my baby!"

"The alternative," he said flatly. "You can take this $20,000 annual salary agreement to work with Edward on the special project. And that lets you keep the baby."

"Are you kidding me?" She was eerily calm. "Are. You. Kidding. Me?" Beneath the calm voice, Mary shook with anger. "All this is about the cocoa plantation? A plantation I have nothing to do with. Something I do not know anything about. I don't even think it is a plantation. I have no information on it at all. For all I know it is a silly joke my friend's grandfather carried on just so they would have an excuse to eat more chocolate. He wants me to work on an old wives' tale in order to keep my own baby?" Her voice was rising now. "This is against the law, I am sure! I will get my own attorney! This is extortion!"

Through the veil of drugged postpartum exhaustion and a curtain of inescapable anxiety, Mary heard Jim pronounce his almighty threat. "Do you have money for that, Mary? The kind of money Edward has?"

Mary's anger slowly collapsed like an imploded house of cards into a pile of wretchedly rampant uncertainty. Her damp eyes closed tight against the room's bright light, where colorful spots floated and bounced chaotically against the darkness behind her lids. It seemed they were reflecting her own delirious fears back to her. Jim waited a few minutes before she opened her defeated eyes and went in for the kill.

"You know that you do not have his kind of money. And you know that people like Edward Burke will always win. Think for a moment, Mary. Think about yourself and think about the baby. You are a beautiful but very young, very single woman. How are you going to work and take care of this child? What man will be interested in a woman with an illegitimate child? You know in your heart your child is better off in a stable home with a mother and a father. Have you thought about that?" His eyebrows rose in question, "My dear, you can't change what has happened. The past is set. But the future is still yours. You are young. You can live your life. Find another man. Have another baby." He extended the pen to her. "Please," he coaxed.

Mary's head throbbed; she was on the verge of throwing up. "Can you give me a moment to think about this, please?"

"If you really want to keep this baby, Edward has offered a very simple solution for you—a very generous and lucrative one too." He gestured, hesitated, and then dramatizing his words, said, "Think of it as a partnership."

Mary's body spontaneously contracted. She gagged and uttered a choking sound, shivering all over.

Jim gazed at her steadily. "It's only chocolate, Mary, and you can have your baby." He stood, turned his back on her. "I'll let you think about it for an hour. The choice is yours." Then he strode quickly out of the room.

Mary turned to stare at the blank wall beside her, overwhelmed. Her first instinctive thought was that she wanted the baby to be taken care of, and she wanted to be the one to do it. She thought of the life they would have, a cute little home, cookies after school, and the two of them reading stories together. How am I supposed to do this? Even with the money, I would be under Edward's dominance for the rest of my life.

Ariel would always be a tool of leverage for him. That is not good for any of us. "Oh!" Mary hit the pillow in her lap out of fear and frustration. "What am I supposed to do?" she cried into the silent room.

After an hour of absorbed contemplation and many tears, Mary knew what her answer would be.

She pushed the call button for the nurse.

"Yes, Mary, can I help you?" the nurse asked sweetly.

"Can you bring the attorney back here?"

"Of course. It looks like he just got back. I'll send him in."

"Thank you," Mary said softly, wiping the tears from her face.

When the door opened, Jim asked straight out, "What have you decided?"

"I want my baby to be loved and cared for," Mary said.

"Yes?" Jim asked with a push for more.

"I want her to have the best chance in life, and I wish I could provide that for her," said Mary with tear-filled eyes.

"That's what we all want for this baby," Jim agreed.

"I am almost twenty." She considered him for a moment. "I only make a small wage, and while your Edward has given me a very generous offer, I know I can't provide the kind of life I would like to be able to give my daughter. I am just a child myself, really."

"That is a very courageous decision, not one to be taken lightly." Once again, he pushed his glasses upward. "It shows your love for the baby, which no one would ever doubt." He extended a pen and contract to Mary. "But Mary, think about it: with the amount he's offered you, you wouldn't have to work except for helping him. You could care for your baby."

As she had thought over her choices, Mary had imagined Edward hovering around, hounding her for information about the cacao trees. Information she did not have. She would be under constant pressure to find it, and the thought of going to Benny, asking for the source of the beans, explaining to him about the baby, it was all too much.

Her eyes focused squarely at Jim as she reached for the paper and pen. Her hands shook. Then she paused. "I cannot help him. I don't know anything. And I need to give the baby the best chance in life. She is the innocent one in this mess and deserves a loving home with parents who are ready to be parents. I am just not ready."

"You are sure about this?"

"As sure as I can be, but can I ask a favor?"

"You can ask me anything... But I can't promise anything."

Mary nodded.

"What's the favor?" Jim queried.

"Can you suggest a name to her parents for me?" Tears broke through the corners of her eyes again. "I've been calling her Ariel."

"I will bring it up to them. But Mary, you can't have anything to do with this child anymore." He carefully lifted Mary's chin to look directly into her eyes. "You must understand that you are not her mother, your name is not on the birth certificate, this adoption is private, and her parents' names will appear on all documentation. Communication between you and them is not permitted in any way—ever."

With a strength built from deep within, Mary looked right back into Jim's eyes and said, "Please, hand me the adoption papers only. You can tell Mister Burke to keep his money."

With that, he extended the pen and papers to Mary.

The pen whispered across the pages. The ink dried quickly, her signature cold and final.

Jim took the document with a nod, unaware of the swirling defiance that simmered in her chest, and shut the door behind him with a soft thud, silence reclaiming its territory.

Mary turned her gaze to the chair beside her, where her colorfully embroidered bag rested. She glanced at the empty doorway before reaching out to the button by her bedside. Her finger pressed it, and a soft chime echoed in the room, breaking the stillness.

Moments later, the nurse appeared, her eyes warm and questioning. "Yes, Miss Mary?"

"Please, bring me my bag." Mary's eyes glistened.

The nurse obliged, placing the worn bag in Mary's lap before stepping back. With fingers defter than their shaking suggested, Mary reached inside, feeling the rough edges of the envelope that Benny had once handed her in secret. The cocoa beans, wrapped in their delicate, age-darkened casing, hummed softly against her palm.

She took the pen she'd held onto from Jim's visit, her heartbeat pulsing with every stroke as she wrote one simple word: Ariel. The ink soaked into the paper, bold and determined.

Mary glanced at the nurse, measuring her trustworthiness, then extended the envelope with a tremor. "Please, I need you to give this to my daughter's adoptive parents. Without anyone else knowing."

The nurse's eyes widened, shifting from the envelope to Mary's tired face, recognizing the unspoken urgency in her request. She nodded slowly, accepting the envelope with a gentleness that promised secrecy.

***

There was something different about Ariel from the very beginning—an intuition that frightened Emily, her adoptive mother.

"I love her, I love her very much," she told her husband, almost like a confession, one morning over breakfast. "But the way she looks at me . . . it's not like when Susan was a baby." Emily was feeding Ariel a bottle at the breakfast table while her older daughter, Susan, was seated next to them, eating cereal.

"Don't be silly," William said, getting up from the table. He kissed the top of Emily's head. "It all happened so quickly that you're probably just in a bit of shock." He reached down, tickling Susan's cheek.

When Emily gave birth to their daughter, Susan, everything had seemed fine. But almost as soon as the midwife handed Susan to Emily, something went wrong.

"I don't feel well," she'd whispered.

William signaled to the midwife, who called for a nurse, who then called for a doctor.

Emily had begun to bleed. As the blood flow increased, Susan was whisked from Emily's arms into William's, and they were quickly ushered out of the room.

"Is she alright? Is she going to be alright?" he pleaded desperately, craning his neck to see what was happening behind him. Emily was hemorrhaging; her life hung in the balance. The doctors and nurses got to work.

"What's happening?" Emily cried, feeling her consciousness ebbing away.

"Shh," a nurse prompted, leaning close to her ear. "The doctors are here."

An anesthesiologist hurried into the room, placing a mask over her face, and she quickly passed out.

When she awoke, William jumped from the chair beside her bed and hovered. "How are you feeling?" he asked.

Emily nodded. "Susan?"

William smiled. "She's fine," he assured her, gesturing to the bassinet in the room. "She's okay," he said with tears in his eyes.

As Susan grew older, William tried to discuss adoption with Emily, but the subject depressed her. The couple wanted another child of their own, several more, but the doctors said that having another baby would pose a terrible risk to Emily's health. So, William and Emily believed their dream of having a big family was over.

***

Susan was five when the phone rang one winter afternoon. It sliced through the household like the cold wind as the outside door opened. The air stung with the kind of chill that clings to your breath, turning it to mist. William's strong arms hefted larger logs; he shifted in the doorway, letting Susan pass through first.

"Almost there, Susie," William encouraged. Her's cheeks flushed pink from the cold, proud to be helping her father carry the logs to the small stack by the hearth. William added a log to the last embers of the morning's fire. The snap of wood and flame was accompanied by a sharper intrusion. A ringing of the phone.

"William here."

"William, it's Jack."

"Hey, Jack. Everything alright?"

"More than alright, I'd say. Listen, I've come across an opportunity that you and Emily might want to consider. . . adoption."

William's breath caught. He glanced down the hall toward Emily's faint silhouette, moving between rooms with fresh laundry. "Adoption?"

"I've recently been informed of a child who might soon need

a family," Jack continued, choosing each word carefully to honor Edward's command for discretion. "It's an unusual circumstance, but one that I believe could be perfect for you both. The child's mother is in a position where she may soon need to make a hard decision. This isn't public knowledge, and for good reason."

He pressed the phone tighter to his ear. "Why us, Jack? How did this come to you?"

Jack paused. "William, you and Emily have been trying for another child for a while now, haven't you? You're good people. The kind who'd step up to this with all the care and love it demands. That's why. And it came through connections that trust us, trust you."

"Does Emily know?"

"Not yet. I wanted to speak to you first, make sure this is something you're prepared to consider. It will need to move quickly, and it comes with the understanding that some details ... they stay with me. It's for the best."

William understood. Jack was the keeper of many secrets, and this one weighed between them now. "Alright, Jack. If this is real, then yes. We'll consider it."

"It's real, William. And it's a chance worth taking. I'll be in touch when things are clearer."

"Thank you, Jack. This means more than you know."

"Oh, I think I know," Jack said softly before the line went quiet and the future, fragile and uncharted, sat between them.

In just three minutes, less time than it took to make a cup of coffee, William's world had shifted, a future unknown but unmistakably set. The details were relayed: the baby, the private plane, the papers. William could almost hear the thrum of the jet engine, feel the bite of wind as it roared to life.

Emily's reaction was a quiet storm when he told her, shock battling hope in the brown of her eyes. "It's what we've always wanted," he whispered, his voice as much a plea as it was reassurance.

"What if the baby's not healthy? What if the mother—" Emily's words contemplating a labyrinth of fears. "I've read about babies being born addicted to drugs. It's heart-wrenching."

William held her close, pressing a kiss to her temple where the scent of lavender lingered from her morning routine. "I promise you, that will not be a problem. The mother is being well cared for throughout the pregnancy. Nothing will go wrong."

She searched his face, her doubt softening but not dissolving. "Is this even legal?" The question hung between them, not out of skepticism but of need, a desire to ensure their joy would be unmarred.

"It's legal, Emily. It's a private adoption. The original family had to step back when they discovered they were having their own child. Everything is in order." His voice was calm, but his mind recalled the sharp, unbending ethics of both his father-in-law and Edward Burke. Men who would build loopholes as readily as empires if it meant a sure outcome.

Weeks passed, in a blur of hushed anticipations. Then one night, as the three sat in the den, sipping hot chocolate, the dice clattering against the Yahtzee board merged with the ringing of the phone.

Emily's father, Jack, greeted her, his voice clipped and steady. "It's time."

"Now?" Emily's breath hitched, her eyes wide, darting to William, then to Susan, who watched them both with the open curiosity only children could manage.

"Right now," the voice on the line confirmed. "The plane is waiting for you at the airport."

Emily set down the receiver, a slow, measured movement. William met her gaze, then turned to their daughter. "We're going to go get your sister now."

***

In the hospital room next to where Mary lay sleeping, Emily and William waited for their new baby. They'd left Susan in Portland, Oregon, with a family friend. An hour passed, then two. "I wonder how much longer it's going to be?" asked Emily, seated on a swivel stool.

"Who knows?" William responded as he slowly paced the floor.

"Can you run to the cafeteria and see if there is anything to snack on?" Emily's question was more of a request based on the anxiety of waiting. Eating would at least give them something to do.

William came back with sandwiches and coffee; still, one more hour passed before a knock on the door finally came. A nurse gently opened the door, carrying the baby wrapped snuggly in a pink blanket. "It's a girl," she announced, handing the tiny bundle to Emily.

Emily sat on the edge of her chair and looked at her new daughter; William stood beside her, petting the baby's soft skin.

"What does Mary look like?" Emily asked him.

"I know just as much as you do—brown hair, blue eyes, 5'3". Do you want to peek in and see her?"

"Yes, I think I would like to do just that," Emily said, handing the baby to him.

She saw the nurse in the hallway and asked, "Excuse me, would it be all right if I saw the birth mother?"

"I don't know; let me ask the doctor," the nurse responded to the unexpected question. A few minutes later, she returned, "Mary's sleeping right now, but if you want to come back later—"

Emily interrupted, "I just want to see what she looks like. I don't want to talk to her."

"Oh," the nurse said, looking around. "Well, I guess you can poke your head in." The nurse quietly opened the door to Mary's room.

There before Emily was the mother of her baby. She was lying under a white sheet, her head resting peacefully on the pillow. Mary's long, deep brown hair framed her face, while her olive skin enhanced her youth. William sidled up beside Emily, and she caught the grateful expression in his eyes upon seeing the beauty before him.

The next afternoon, Emily and William and their attorney met with the attorney in charge of the adoption, who presented paperwork across a table in their conference room at the hospital. "Mary signed all of the documents yesterday, so you are now the baby's parents, pending the court's signature, of course," he said. "We will file the adoption in Oregon. Until the courts have officially filed this adoption, the baby will technically be considered a ward of the state—Oregon, in this case. Your names will be on her birth certificate when it is official."

"But there is one thing Mary wanted to ask," the attorney

said. "She wanted to name the baby."

"We've already chosen a name," William said.

"When I spoke with Mary earlier, I didn't get the impression that she was trying to step on your toes. She just wanted to give the baby something to ease her own closure."

Emily was quiet for a moment, and when William was about to speak, she placed her hand on his forearm to stop him. Emily's voice was soft. "What name did she have in mind?"

"Ariel," Jim said.

"Ariel." Emily looked at William quietly then said, "I can understand the closure Mary needs. No matter how all this happened or the poor choices she made, in the end she did what was right. So, I think we can at least do this for her. It's just a name. We have our baby, and Ariel will never know any different."

The hallway outside the maternity ward was filled with the usual echoes of quiet conversations, the squeak of shoes on polished tiles, and the steady beep of distant monitors. William held the baby close, his arm gently guiding Emily as they moved toward the exit. The weight of this moment pressed on them—not just the newness of their daughter, but the uncharted life waiting beyond these walls.

Just as they reached the double doors, a nurse in a crisp

uniform stepped forward, hesitating for a fraction of a moment before calling out.

"Excuse me, Mr. and Mrs.?" Her voice was soft but insistent, enough to halt their steps. William turned, his eyes meeting hers with the practiced alertness of a man prepared for sudden news. The nurse's gaze dropped briefly to the bundle in his arms, and her expression shifted from clinical professionalism to something warmer, more personal.

"Yes?" Emily responded, shifting her weight to see the nurse better, her curiosity piqued by the nurse's expression.

"I'm sorry to stop you like this, but there's something important. It's from Mary—the baby's... mother," the nurse said, pulling a small, plain envelope from the pocket of her uniform. She held it out to them.

William exchanged a glance with Emily, his arms instinctively holding the baby closer as he reached for the envelope. The nurse didn't let go immediately, her eyes pleading for understanding.

"She wanted me to tell you that it's ... special. The beans inside—they were something she held dear. She said they'd bring ... Well, she said they were a gift that should stay with the child. It would mean a lot if you kept them."

Emily's expression was confused. "But this is my baby, not hers. She didn't want it." Her eyes darted from the nurse to her husband. "Why does she keep interjecting herself? She needs to let go."

William looked at the nurse, taking in the seriousness of her expression, the way she hovered, unsure whether her mission had been completed as intended.

"We'll take them," he said, voice steady, even though he questioned what they'd do with them.

The nurse's shoulders relaxed, the lines of tension easing from her face. "Thank you," she whispered, stepping back as they turned once more toward the exit, this time with the envelope tucked safely in William's coat pocket.

* * *

It didn't matter how Ariel had come to be part of their family, or whether the glimmer in her eyes that Emily thought she saw was real or imagined. What truly mattered was the boundless love Emily felt. A love that transcended her quiet longing to have been Ariel's birth mother. In time, that love deepened until, Ariel became as much her daughter as Susan was.

Ariel grew into a quiet girl, which no one would have guessed during the first year of her life when she screamed constantly. The only time she didn't cry in that first year was when she was rocked in William's arms. William had an undying love for Susan and Emily, but when he held Ariel, he felt something so remarkable that it nearly took his breath away.

"Sometimes I think you love her more than me," Emily said offhandedly one day, watching William as he walked around the house holding the baby.

William looked up. "That's impossible," he reassured his wife.

Chapter Nine

Without the proper attention, without love, chocolate becomes very dry and brittle, eventually becoming a dull, almost lifeless powder.

* * *

Returning from a walk to stretch my legs after my dinner, which was pushed more around the plate with the back of my fork than eaten, I was ready for bed—well, ready to recline the airplane chair. The flight attendant laid a thinly quilted blanket over me.

Damion had already dozed off, along with both Melony and Harvey.

"Thank you, Madge," I said.

"Thank you for sharing the story. Pleasant dreams," she said, her voice a whisper.

"Good night."

Exhaustion overtook me just as a curious little voice pushed its way to the forefront of my mind, as if no time had passed. Kites soared in the wind, almost as free as the seagulls, and she and her father sat on driftwood, holding the strings. How so very long ago that seemed now. So long ago it was merely a dream.

* * *

"Susan?" Ariel asked, standing at her sister's doorway. "Can you spell something for me and show me how to write it?"

"What do you want to know?" Susan said, looking up from her homework.

"Oh, just a word," Ariel said, trying not to draw attention to what she had in mind. Which only made her look more suspicious.

"What word?" Susan asked, coaxing Ariel to get on with what she wanted.

"Flower," Ariel said quietly.

"Flower?" Susan repeated.

Ariel nodded, then said, "and Dear and Lady."

"That's three words. What do you need them for?" Susan's interest was piqued.

"I just need to write a letter to someone, and I have to mail it today, so I need to know those words," Ariel explained.

"You will need to know how to write the other words in your letter, too, right?" Susan confirmed her curiosity as to what the other words would be.

"Yeah, but she will be able to read my writing. I have special cursive," Ariel said in her most ladylike manner, as though she'd been writing cursive for years already, at age three.

"Then just use that cursive to write the words you just asked for." Susan sheepishly smiled.

"Well, because those words are special. They are really important, and I need to mail my letter before it gets dark. Can you help me?"

"Of course. Come here."

Ariel stepped into the room and walked over to Susan's desk.

"Okay, sit in my chair." Susan directed.

Ariel climbed into the chair, sitting on her knees giving her an extra boost. "This is how you hold a pencil." Susan put the pencil in Ariel's hand and moved her little fingers into place. "Now, I am going to move your hand to move the pencil to spell the words, okay?"

"Okay," Ariel said with contained excitement.

"Good job. This says, Dear Lady Flower." Susan pointed to each word as she read them.

"What if I need to say, Dear Flower Lady?" Ariel asked.

"That is easy. When you write words, you write them in the same order you speak them. So just switch the lady and the flower."

"Thanks, Susan. Can you write them for me that way, too, in your kind of writing?"

"Yep, and then you can trace them." Susan gave Ariel several pieces of paper and showed her how to put one piece over the words she wrote in black marker and how to trace them.

Ariel skipped back to her own room, sat at her own desk, and began her tracing practice with the magic pencil Susan gave her that would help her stay in the lines and help her learn to write even more words.

The mailing of that first letter was a day or so late while Ariel practiced. It was posted in a glass jar she took from her mother's sewing basket and then buried in a clearing in the pine trees, a secret garden hideaway. The letters she'd mail there were important, and the Flower Lady would read them all.

Over the next few months, Susan sat with Ariel teaching her about the dictionary, how it works and how to sound out letters to make the words she was looking for. And explained that spelling more complicated words was a little trickier because you can't sound them out the way they were practicing.

"Over time, Ariel, you will know how to spell most of them," Susan explained.

"Okay, what if I need to know what the words for the dots are?" Ariel asked.

"Like the periods and question marks?" Susan asked.

"No, like the dots we are made of." Ariel lifted her hand to show Susan all the creases in her skin. "If you look really close, they are see-through." She rubbed her fingers together as if feeling them there, the fine motes of warmth suspended between skin and air.

"Ariel, not this again. You are not see-through," Susan said, her tone thinning the air. She stood up. "Why do you keep saying this? Why do you keep talking like this? Is this what you are writing about?"

Ariel didn't say anything for a minute, then said, "Haven't you noticed we are all put together like a sheet, and that we weave into the places we go? We aren't just people, Susan. And I need to tell the Flower Lady about these discoveries. It is important," Ariel explained. "She wants to know."

"Ariel, don't tell anyone else what you just told me, okay?" Susan explained. "People don't want to hear all this kind of stuff you say. You won't have any friends. People are just going to think you are weird. Why don't you just go play with dolls or something?"

"I don't like dolls. They aren't real babies; they are just pretend. And this is important. This is not pretending, Susan. There is more stuff I want to tell the Flower Lady, too. She likes reading my letters." Ariel took a breath. "Where can I find how to spell the words that have this stuff? The dots just keep going and they talk to each other, and they have smaller squiggle ladders, and the smaller squiggle ladders have smaller squiggle ladders, and it keeps going. Isn't that important? It is the secret." Susan just looked at Ariel wide-eyed as she continued. "And at night, I go way out into space, and all that darkness we see when we look up is filled with amazing things. And if you go far enough away, you go home. But you don't even have to go anywhere because we are already home. I learned that it wasn't me travelling into space, it was me just not looking through my eyes on my head. Everything our eyes can't see is all around us right now. Do you see it?"

"Ariel, you are almost four years old. It is time to put this imaginary game away. You are getting too big for it." Susan turned Ariel's shoulders and walked her out of her room. "Don't talk like this to people. It makes them feel weird. And what are you doing with all these letters you're writing?"

"Fine. I won't say anything," Ariel's gaze lowered, turning inward, following the quiet path from her heart toward the Land of Ought Not, where the Flower Lady was tucked away. *And I am not saying where I bury the letters either, because they need to stay safe,* she thought.

* * *

Once upon a time, there was a forest older than the memory of men, and in its quietest depths, where the light of the sun only whispered, stood a shack. Its wooden walls leaned like an old man against the wind. Moss painted its edges, and ivy climbed like forgotten secrets, wrapping around the windows, protecting the mysteries inside.

Ariel was only four years old when her small, wandering feet brought her to the edge of this place. She had been following the soft melody of a bird, its song bright, like sunlight breaking through storm clouds. It guided her through trees taller than dreams and past brooks that gurgled with laughter at her naked feet.

At the edge of a clearing, through the thick of ferns and branches, she saw it. The shack. It was a shadow out of place in the green. Ariel froze, her heart beating as fast as a moth's wings. She wasn't sure if the place belonged to a friend or a monster, but it felt important—like the first word of a story waiting to be written.

She crept closer, her small hands brushing the bark of trees, asking for their permission. The air smelled of secrets buried too deep for anyone to dig. She peeked through a crack in the door. Dust motes spun in the stillness, a dance for no one. Inside, there was nothing but emptiness. An emptiness that invited her.

Ariel stepped back and looked around, her little mind spinning. This shack felt like a place no one had found in a very long time. It felt like it belonged to the "Ought Not," the things that crept past the edges of rules and calendars, the things that whispered to her when the world was quiet.

She knelt down, her fingers brushing the dirt at the shack's feet. There, she dug her first hole. Just deep enough for what she needed it for. From her knapsack, she pulled a glass jar that had once held strawberry jam. Inside was a simple letter, written in shaky block letters on a torn scrap of paper:

Dear Flower Lady,

Thank you for believing in me. I believe in you too.

From, Ariel

She buried it with the solemnity of planting a seed. The earth closed over the jar, it had been waiting for her words.

And so, the shack became hers, a place she would return to again and again, year after year, with jars filled with thoughts too big for her small frame to carry. It became her map to the

Land of Ought Not, her refuge from the heavy world of what ought to be.

And though she didn't know it yet, the shack had been waiting for her, too.

* * *

Just before Ariel's fifth birthday, William and Emily returned from their travels, their arms filled with small tokens of faraway places. Ariel listened about a world she had yet to know. Amid the trinkets and tales, Emily gently placed a package in front of Ariel, wrapped in crisp, ivory paper with a velvety blue ribbon.

"Go on, sweetheart," Emily said, her voice soft. William watched with a quiet smile, his hands resting on Emily's shoulders.

Ariel reached out and took the package. She loosened the bow, the paper crinkling as it fell away, revealing a china doll wearing a brown, flower-patterned dress. Its hair was dark, the same deep chestnut as Ariel's own, and its hazel eyes looked upon her with unspoken recognition. A small key protruded from the doll's back, waiting to be wound.

"It plays a song," William said, leaning down to show her how to turn the key. A few gentle twists and the soft, wistful strains of "Lara's Theme" began to fill the room.

Ariel's heart clenched with an odd fluttering she couldn't

name. She rarely played with toys, their purpose always unclear, why did they get her a doll? Disappointment held her in place. What was she supposed to do now? She couldn't give it back, because the doll seemed to ask something of her.

"Why this?" she whispered, barely loud enough for her parents to hear.

Emily's eyes softened, the tenderness deepening. "Because it reminded us of you. Something precious, to cherish and care for."

Ariel considered the doll, looking into her eyes, caressing her tiny hands, feeling the delicate fingers, *She has brown and orange eyes like me, and our hair is the same.* Turning to carry it up stairs. Her fingers brushing the porcelain cheek before placing the doll on the little rocking chair opposite her bed. There it sat, unmoving, days turned into weeks and weeks into a year. For that year, every glance at the doll stirred a feeling she couldn't quite name, a responsibility that sat in that chair patiently trading glances with her. And, Ariel did her best to ignore it.

"Was it the same when I came out of your tummy?" the newly six-year-old Ariel asked her mother when her baby brother was born.

"No, you weren't in my tummy. We got you at the hospital when you were ready to come home."

Ariel thought about that for a minute. "Well, where did I come from then? Is there a place at the hospital, a garden for babies?"

"You grew inside a different woman."

"I was inside a different mommy? So"—Ariel calculated the information—"so, I have a different mom? Why am I not with her?"

"I'm your mom," Emily said reassuringly.

"I know you're my mom. But how did you get me? Why doesn't my real mom have me? Is a different mommy going to take this baby?" Ariel pointed at the crib.

"No, no one is going to take your brother, and no one is taking you either," Emily said.

"So... anybody can be my mom. But not anybody can be his? So, that means I am not real, that I am pretend. I have to pretend I am real." But, seeing Emily's reaction to her questions, Ariel decided to refrain from asking any more until later that night.

When the house was quiet, Ariel slipped from her covers and walked into her dad's office, where he worked in the evenings.

"Daddy?" she asked as she made her way to him while pretending the slats of the oak floor were balance beams.

"You should be sleeping," he said.

She stood next to him.

"Daddy, do you know who my real mom is?" Ariel asked nonchalantly.

"Ariel, we are your parents. You are my daughter."

The way he said it, she believed him. She wanted to be real.

"I mean, do you know whose tummy I came from?" She rephrased her question.

William picked Ariel up, sitting her on his lap. "She was a young lady who couldn't take care of you, so she gave you to us."

"Is Susan real like the baby, or is she pretend like me?"

"Susan is our natural daughter, but you are all our real children."

But I'm borrowed, Ariel thought.

They sat quietly while her brain counted along with the second hand of the clock; *Tick. Tock. Tick. Tock. Tick. Tock.* She snuggled into her father's chest. *Tick. Tock.*

"What was she like? Did you see her?" Ariel asked into the rhythm.

"I've seen her picture. But you don't need to worry about this. It doesn't change anything," he told her reassuringly.

Her brain stopped following the clock. "Can I see it?" she asked. "Her picture?"

"It's time for bed now. But one day, I will show you her picture," he said, standing her back onto the floor.

"Okay, I can wait. I love you. I know you are my dad, and Mom is my mom. I just wanted to see where I started from."

Months skipped forward like the turning of a hand-drawn flipbook, each moment blurring into the next until one golden afternoon. The sunlight spilled through the windows of Ariel's bedroom in soft, slanting beams, painting the walls around the little chair. Ariel stood still, her gaze following the sunlight to where the doll had sat so patiently for twelve months.

"Fine." She answered the doll's questioning stare.

Ariel crossed her arms and walked deliberately across the room. She reached for the doll, whom she named Kitty Flower, and cradled it close against her chest. Kitty's porcelain face rested lightly against Ariel's shoulder, and the room exhaled around them.

In that single moment, the path from her heart to the land of Ought Not opened, and the two of them went through the gates as a realization hit, love was not just something given—it was something chosen. And she chose now, with all the clarity her young heart could muster, to give her love to Kitty.

From that day forward, Ariel and Kitty were inseparable. Kitty, in her brown flowered dress, became a keeper of secrets, a bearer of burdens, and the quiet guardian of Ariel's heart. Perhaps it sounds like the sort of tale told too many times, but Kitty truly held something no one else could: the most fragile, most precious parts of Ariel's soul.

Every tear that Ariel shed, Kitty absorbed into her soft cotton body. Every whispered thought, every fleeting hope, every moment of loneliness—Kitty held them all. Ariel had learned early on that love, when exposed to the wrong hands, could be twisted into a weapon. But Kitty would never betray her, not in words, not in silence. Their bond was a sanctuary.

And within this sanctuary was a secret: the fairytale, the land of Ought Not.

It began, as all the best tales do, in fragments and glimpses. Pieces of it drifted into Ariel's mind, like autumn leaves carried on a breeze. Once, it blew in during a quiet exchange between her parents as they drove along a winding road. The tires humming softly against the pavement, the rhythm lulling Ariel into a half-dream as she stared out the window.

She wasn't meant to catch the words, but her ears were keen. "Faith," her mother said, her voice carrying the hopeful lilt they could bring it into their lives. Her father replied with the idea weighed him down. The word "church" wove into their conversation, foreign and intriguing to Ariel.

Feeling bold, she leaned forward from her spot in the backseat. "I have faith!" she declared, her announcement bright and earnest.

Her mother turned, a glimmer of surprise and triumph in her eyes. But before the moment could rest, Ariel added with a burst of unrestrained relief to share, "I have faith in chocolate!" and in a second breath, since they were on the subject of faith, she added, "Also, who are people that can give a message to my mom so I can say thank you for not killing me."

Her parents' eyes grew like saucers. Emily closed hers eyes for an extended second while drawing breath. "What did you say?" She asked.

"Well, you told me my mom wanted to get rid of me and then she didn't. And that is why I am here. And, well, so, I think I should at least say thank you."

William shot a glance to Emily. Emily sighed. "I never said that, Ariel. And, you can't have faith in chocolate. It's just chocolate."

"No," Ariel insisted, her hazel eyes glowing with conviction. "My chocolate is special. It is like going home. It makes things easier to understand. It's magic."

Her mother opened her mouth to reply but stopped. Ariel's

gaze had turned distant; she was no longer in the car. She was back on the Oregon coast, standing amidst the pounding surf, where the air was heavy with salt, and a fine mist turned into steady rain as dark clouds gathered overhead. Giant rocks loomed like ancient guardians against the relentless waves. In that stormy memory, Ariel had tasted chocolate for the first time, a single bite melting on her tongue, rich and bittersweet. The warmth of it had spread through her like the glow of a lantern in the night, quieting the chaos of the storm.

That was when she first understood: chocolate wasn't just chocolate. It was a bridge, connecting her to something unnamable.

Returning to the present, Ariel blinked." You don't understand," she said softly, there was no frustration in her voice—only wonder.

Her mother and father exchanged a glance, neither knowing how to respond. For the rest of the drive, Ariel cradled Kitty on her lap, stroking the doll's soft dress. And though she didn't speak again, her mind wandered back to the fairy tale, piecing together the magic that only she could see, back to her first taste.

* * *

"What's that?" asked Ariel, pointing down from the outcrop. She was dressed in Susan's bright yellow slicker, which draped over her yellow rain pants all the way to the ankles of her little black rain boots.

William held her hand and turned his attention to the pounding surf below where she pointed. "That's the Pacific Ocean," he said, gently squeezing her hand a few times. The waves crashing into the rocks hypnotized her.

"Is the water wild on the bottom of the ocean?" Her eyes stretched the thought beneath the waves, searching for the sand. "Does rock you under the water? Where do the fish go in a storm? Do they get smashed on the rocks?" "What if we took the dinghy out there?" she asked. "Would we die? Does it hurt to die?" She paused, searching his face. "Can I be afraid to die and not be, at the same time?"

"Come on," William said, lifting her in one motion, drawing her into his arms. "Let's go." The scent of sea or damp wool embedded that cliff within her, the moment she first understood the ocean's power, and her father's almost equal love.

On their way back to the beach house, Ariel and William stopped at the small market to pick up a few things Emily needed for dinner. As they hiked through the dunes, Ariel's hands ran along the grass, shaking water from the blades. They stepped out of the soft sand and into the deep moist woods, their shoes crunching gravel beneath them. As she scampered along the damp paths, Susan's bright yellow slicker felt like a royal cape.

"I'd like to teach . . . the world to sing . . .in perfect harmony

... with apple trees ... and honeybees ... and snow-white turtle doves," she sang, her small voice rising high above with the birds. Raindrops landed in the trees, rolling through a labyrinth of leaves before cascading down upon them.

She kicked through puddles and jumped over fallen branches. The slicker billowed as she twirled off a log. The bottom hem floated upward, turning into fairy wings, lifting her to soar and weave about the evergreen canopy. Landing on the edge of a bird's nest, she looked around. In the distance, the ocean rolled over the sand, crabs scurried into holes, and the dune grasses bowed toward her perch. She jumped to play with ladybugs and awakened the fireflies. She laughed, somersaulting freely; her delicate, dragonfly-like wings brought her down, carefully setting her feet on the floor just as the house came into view.

Her father slowed, removing something not from one of the grocery bags but from his pocket. It was wrapped in parchment and twine. "Try this." His offer was laced with intrigue.

"What is it?" she asked, taking the piece of candy and turning it over curiously. She brought it in for a better look.

"It is chocolate," he watched her, "for you."

Earthy aromas caused her mouth to water. The rolled sleeves of the oversized rain slicker exposed her hands with the stretch of her arms. Her shoulder gave a little shrug, and as her teeth bit into a corner it turned to silk, melting into her mouth. Her eyes alighted. Mirroring her father's gaze. Then a wave, a deep earthy presence connected her heart from beyond and her small toes wiggled in the little black rain boots.

Love.

In her mind, time stood still. Even then, at three years old, comfort attached itself to a memory floating just out of reach.

* * *

"Ariel," her mother said from the front seat of the car, snapping her back into the present. "You don't have special chocolate. You eat the same kind we all do."

"Okay," Ariel said, not wanting to explain, and gazed back out the window where her soul glided towards images of harvest fairies leading her through the trees, where their fairy pod homes adorned the trunks. Where cocoa simmered over a fire and sparks danced with rich intoxicating vapor seeping into the dark, star-studded sky.

Chapter Ten

The summer wind curled through the open study window, carrying the scent of pine and ink-drenched paper. Ariel sat cross-legged on the floor, her fingers tracing the raised edges of the carpet's pattern as she listened.

"...the market's shifting, Jack," William said. "The steel industry's softening. We move now, we win."

Jack Burke exhaled, the ice in his glass clinking as he swirled his drink. "And what about the sugar trade? It's not just for candy—cocoa futures, corn syrup—they're essentials."

Ariel's ears perked up. *Cocoa.* She barely understood the conversation, but something in the way her grandfather spoke made her stomach flutter. Essentials.

She peeked over the edge of the desk. William caught the movement and turned sharply. "Ariel, this isn't a game. Run along."

She did—but not to play.

The newspaper smelled of ink and coffee as Ariel flattened the business section on the kitchen table. Numbers lined the columns like puzzle pieces waiting to be solved. She didn't know all the rules yet, but knew this much—people studied this paper to make money.

Taking the change she had been gathering—pennies from sidewalks, nickles and dimes beneath the sofa cusions, she walked into the drugstore and bought a handful of penny candy.

At a wedding reception across the street, she approached adults in front lawn. "Rare jelly beans. Five cents," she said, from the hedgerows, her voice steady.

A quarter clinked into her palm.

Her first profit. And, on to the next.

The old manor rose at the end of a winding drive, its weathered stone draped in ivy and wisteria, whispering secrets in the breeze. Ariel stood at the threshold, counting her fingers repetitive taps as scents of vanilla and lemon zest drifted from Mrs.' kitchen.

"Mrs. Briggs," she began, her voice small, teetering on the edge of retreat, "My name is Ariel, I live up the lane. I was wondering... do you have any work I could do? Anything I can help with?" Please, I'm not bad. Please don't turn me away. she thought, the old ache of not being enough clawing at her.

The woman wiped flour from her hands onto a linen apron, considering Ariel. "Work, dear? There's always something here." She opened the door for Ariel to come in, and set a heavy recipe book on the worn oak table. "Start with this—read for me. My eyes aren't what they used to be."

"Out loud?" Ariel's pulse jolted, a trapped bird seeking a window.

"It'll be fine," Mrs. Briggs said, her tone a steady anchor. "Take your time."

Ariel sat, brushing flour from the page. Her throat cinching. Oh, please know how to read. She begged her brain. "Mrs. Briggs..." she faltered, "can I... close my eyes to read?"

The old woman's hands, lined with time, stilled. "Close your eyes?"

Ariel nodded uneasily, waiting for a reprimand. "It helps."

Mrs. Briggs said nothing for a moment. Then, as if this were the most ordinary request in the world, she slid the book closer. "Go on, then."

Ariel let her gaze sweep over the page—quick as lightning, afraid the words would scatter if she looked too long. Then she shut her eyes. Cold, soft snow and granular sand emerged, both white. A sprinkle of the sea, a taste repugnant in mass.

A breath. The warmth of the kitchen wrapped around her like a shawl.

"Three cups of sifted flour," she murmured. "One cup of sugar. A pinch of salt." A cow and milkmaid, a churn in action. "Butter. A half cup. And yeast."

Mrs. Briggs said nothing at first. Then a slow, knowing smile spread across her lips. "Well now," she said softly, "isn't that something."

They baked in quietly after that, rolling dough into perfect rounds, dusting sugar over the tops. When the cookies were golden and warm, Mrs. Briggs poured them each a cup of tea, and they sat by the window watching the squirrels dart across the garden wall.

Ariel cupped the warm porcelain in her hands, the scent of bergamot curling into the air. "You remind me of the Flower Lady," she said suddenly.

Mrs. Briggs turned, amusement glinting in her eyes. "Do I now? And who might that be?"

Ariel hesitated, then smiled to herself. "Just someone who understands the quiet things."

Mrs. Briggs studied her for a long moment, then reached into her apron pocket, pulling out a crisp five-dollar bill. She folded it into Ariel's palm.

By winter, Ariel had been through dozens of newspaper pages and was beginning to understand. One name stood out—Disney.

She found the number for a stockbroker.

"I'd like to buy Disney stock please," she said, gripping the receiver tightly.

There was a pause, then a chuckle. "That's great, kid. Why don't you talk to your parents about it?"

Ariel did. At the dinner table, she laid out her plan, her earnings from the candy venture stacked neatly in front of her. "I think it is a good time to buy it," she said. "and I can buy $25.00 at .49 cents. That will be about 51 shares. Right? I wanted to buy a chocolate company but couldn't find one. But Disneyland has chocolate. "

William glanced at the coins and dollar bills before narrowing his eyes. "Where'd you get twenty-five dollars?"

Ariel straightened. "Picking apples and stuff."

William's jaw tightened, an ever so slight clench. He nodded, slow and measured, but his fingers tapped against the table. "You've been knocking on doors?"

His fingers stopped tapping.

She hurried on. "I even help Mrs. Briggs making cookies. She is who I do the most for."

"That's enough," Red flashed across her father's eyes. Disappointment in her. Disbelief of her audacity.

The sharpness in his voice cut her off. He picked up his fork, then set it down.

Is Mrs. Briggs in trouble? I'm sorry Mrs. Briggs. Ariel swallowed back the question, while another still on her tongue trekked on. She pushed a coin against the stack with her finger, aligning it just so.

"...Could you help me buy the stock?" Her voice was soft, almost an afterthought.

William didn't look up right away from his plate, rather, he wiped his mouth with his napkin, set it down, and let out a slow breath through his nose. Then, and only then did he glance at her.

"Fine."

It was a simple word.

Success. Though part of her suspected otherwise.

***

For Ariel, nature was a place of fascination and worship, a place of joy and knowledge. Intuitively, she was in sync with

William's feelings about organized religion. Her father's refusal to attend church was a great gift for Ariel. Instead of sitting in a stuffy room on Sunday mornings, listening to some adult drone on about what she should think and believe, she found herself in the swimming pool with her father.

For her, there were few things more magical than floating in the shimmering clarity of the heated pool, once she had coaxed her body into the water, that is. Below the surface, she was a mermaid, and flowers swayed in the current like a dance over the autumn leaves. Then she'd breach as a whale into the pale blue sky, and Ariel felt alive.

"Ariel, why don't you get ready to go? I only have a few more laps before I am done," her father called out over the pool.

"Okay, Dad!" She was excited for a hot dog and fresh-cut fries with poppy seeds, as was their special tradition on after-the-pool Sunday mornings.

Dressed in her navy and red sweat suit, Ariel waited for William, pacing the floor and following the lines between the tiles. "Step on a crack and break your back," she repeated, trying to avoid the cracks.

"Ready to go?" William's words caught her attention.

"Yep!" she said, skipping over and taking his hand as they walked through the parking lot to the silver Mercedes convertible.

"It's just like Wonder Woman's car, you know, Dad!" she said, buckling her seat belt.

"Just the same." The ignition turned over; they were off.

At the deli, Ariel held the door open for her dad and then skirted around him to the counter, where she stood on her tiptoes just because she liked the feeling of being a few inches taller at the order counter.

"Can you please give me some vinegar, too, please?" she asked the man in the red- and white-striped apron.

"Sure thing, sweetie," he said, flashing her a cigarette-stained smile. "How was your swim?"

"It was good. How is the hot dog business today?" She leaned forward, trying to catch a glimpse into the kitchen.

"It's pretty busy—"

"She doesn't want any vinegar," William interrupted.

"I would like to try some today, Dad. Remember, Susan likes it on her French fries?"

"I just said you don't want any, Ariel." William's voice was flat and firm.

"But Dad, I want to . . ." His eyes stopped her request. "Oh, never mind."

"You sure?" the man in the stripes asked. "I hear it's what they do in Europe."

"And on Wall Street?" Numbers flew through the air. "Who owns the vinegar company? Maybe you should buy it. A lot of people eat vinegar, you know," Ariel said.

The man in the stripes laughed. "I'll need to sell a few more hot dogs first, but I'll let you know when I am ready—"

Once again, William interrupted, "She is sure she doesn't want vinegar."

Arriving home, Ariel hopped out of the car, ready to play.

"Thanks for lunch, Dad!"

"Wait for me," he said.

In the mudroom, her finger traced the wooden Morris the Moose coat rack when a vice grabbed her shoulders, lifting her from the ground. Her cheek stung as it hit the cold rock wall. And once again—slam.

"Don't ever. Contradict me. Again." Quiet words hissed with venom, dropping her to the floor. Then it was gone.

She waited.

Tears welled, watching her father go back toward the garage.

Dusting the top of her shoes, her fingers traced the stitching of her Mary Janes, until her heart settled and she could find Emily.

"Hi, honey, how was your swim?" her mother asked.

Through the window, Mt. Hood majestically stood on the horizon on the rare bright blue day.

"Good... But Dad..." Ariel started.

Putting her needlepoint down, Emily asked Ariel, "Dad what?"

"Dad just..."

A shadow moved into the doorway.

"Ariel, let's get your suit and towel put away," William said as if nothing had happened.

Ariel turned and obeyed.

Once she had found safety in her father's arms; now something tense, something combative lurked behind his eyes, brewing at her questions, increasing in anger. Squeezing her. Shaking her.

What did I do? Ariel asked herself, understanding that question held far more weight than four simple words.

Ariel watched her father closely, the way a sailor watches

the sea. Its beauty, its strength, but also its capacity for storms. William was a man of two faces—one familiar and kind, the father she adored, who flew kites at the beach and bought her chocolate. But beneath that face, another lurked: a monster born from a pain so deep it spilled into his actions, staining the quiet spaces of their home.

Dr. Jekyll and Mr. Hyde. Ariel didn't need the story to understand the truth of it. She lived it.

His anger was not loud and explosive but quiet, simmering like liquid heat, seeping through the cracks of his carefully curated facade. It burned in small, precise ways, unpredictable as a flame catching stray threads. Over time, Ariel learned to anticipate it. She learned what it meant to walk on eggshells long before she ever heard the phrase.

Her days became a study in reading signs, her home an emotional weather map. William's face was the barometer, his movements the shifting winds. She trained herself to search for signals—the furrow of his brow, the tension in his jaw, the set of his shoulders. The wrong tone, a misplaced question, a single glance could be the storm's warning.

It wasn't just her father. Ariel watched everyone, searching the backs of their eyes for hidden truths. She could tell, in an instant, who someone really was, or at least who they were in that moment. It became her survival skill, a gift and a curse.

When she thought the house was safe, Ariel would roam its corners, searching for fragments of love and hope. She found them in old letters between her parents, the ones that spoke of a time before things became complicated. She traced her fingers over photographs, memorizing the faces of her family, their smiles frozen in time. Emily's needlework pillows and linens, with their soft, intricate patterns, became symbols of a world that could still be beautiful.

But mistakes were dangerous. If Ariel made one—spilled a glass of water, made the wrong facial expression . . . (She practiced proper facial expressions in the mirror because she was always asked what was wrong with her face.) Maybe she left a door ajar—it was as though the entire world turned to glass beneath her feet. She'd freeze, paralyzed by fear, every movement calculated to avoid further cracks. Over time, she decided it was better not to be seen at all.

* * *

Her family's home was just up the lane from a magnificent state park with lush foliage and streams, and where the withered old shack that [RA1] leaned very slightly, tired from age. Playing alone in the forest was forbidden, so she devised a way to play without too many traces of mischief. Stripping off her everyday play clothes, she donned clothing in a plastic bag buried in her secret garden. Her "forest" clothes were ragged, and her hair became mussed with moss and bark as the days went on. Her eyes glistened like diamonds from behind a dirt-encrusted face. With her doll Kitty, they'd explore the forest, roast beaked hazelnuts in mini campfires, and sang amongst the din of wildlife. Whenever something larger than a squirrel crackled leaves around them, they'd slip into the thickets and hide. Ariel explored the outer realms of the world, bathed in natural pools of light, tried to tame animals, and ate berries off bushes along the trail. The woman, the Flower Lady, to whom she wrote, lived in the forest. Although, when she showed up, the forest changed to an unknown location. The Flower Lady loved silence as much as Ariel, because inside the silence was melody.

It was here, in this space, where time stopped. Where the breath in Ariel's lungs settled comfortably in the space between inhale and exhale. Where the edge of the universe softened and life hovered, all-encompassing, simultaneously the deepest darkness and brighter than the sun. And in the middle, chocolate warmed over low flames.

Chapter Eleven

1981

Giant fires roared, heating the old English-style manor where a now eleven-year-old Ariel sipped hot water, warming up in her parents' library. An instinctive desire to explore the unknown had taken her to the door of her father's attic study earlier that day. The garret, primarily unfinished, ran like a wide corridor. Outside, wind and rain pelted the windows. Her ears searched for the sounds of the car. Behind the door, the musty smell of old wood and books held tightly to their secrets. To her right, a rickety ladder led to the upper mezzanine of family storage, under which she fumbled for the light switch; a spider web brushed the back of her hand. Light quickly flooded the darkness.

Propping the door open, her slipper stood guard as she made her way toward her father's desk sitting beneath the small window showing off the grey Oregon sky; taxidermies of pheasant and quail hung on either side.

"Nobody wants you here, Ariel. You're a dumb weirdo, and you ruin people's lives." Her younger brother's words burned through her mind, carving deep into the space where she stored things she wished she could forget.

"Why can't I just be normal? Why am I so stupid? Why can't I just be real?"

"Fine." The word acquiesced the pondering. A yielding truce to something she couldn't change. But the word morphed into her father. And now she knew what she wanted to find now.

To see the stock certificates.

"Dad?" she asked, keeping her voice soft "Can you explain stock certificates again?"

He hadn't looked up from his book. "We've talked about this before."

"I know," she had said quickly, "but I was thinking about how they prove ownership, like... a receipt, right?"

His brow flicked up, just barely, but she pressed on. "And when you buy stocks for someone—like if you bought them for me—would the certificates be in my name? Or yours?"

The silence had stretched between them, taut, heavy.

"Could I... see them?"

William had closed his book. Slowly.

"That's enough," he had said. Firm. Final.

And that had been the end of it.

But not for her.

Now, standing in the hush of his study, her fingers curled around the handle of the locked drawer, the air humming with a quiet, pulsing urgency.

A key had to be somewhere.

Maybe in his desk. Maybe behind the bookshelves. Maybe hidden in plain sight.

Maybe, just maybe, she would finally have proof.

Proof that she wasn't stupid.

Proof that she wasn't imagining things.

Proof something was real.

She thought while she opened the first few drawers of her father's file cabinet. Nothing caught her attention, though, just paperwork for her father's business. The bottom drawer, however, was locked.

Her fingers drummed.

"No one goes into my office. You got that?" His words whispered with the wind. She bit her lower lip. Well, for all I know, forbidden places may hold answers to questions. She scanned the room for the key's perfect hiding place. I bet he didn't hide them because no one goes into his office.

Three small keys dwelt amongst silver paperclips in the desk's top drawer.

Oh, one of you, please work. The second key did the trick. Most files held recognizable names, and a daily, weekly, monthly, and yearly record of how many miles her father had run and his monthly cholesterol counts, blood pressure, and other medical records, which he monitored obsessively. He was the pillar of health and as near to Jack LaLanne as one could get. Ariel thumbed through the folders, stopping on her name. Checking over her shoulder, she pulled it out.

Announcements of adoption, little drawings for Father's Day, old report cards, and . . . what's that? Her name in cursive she didn't recognize on an envelope. It bulged. She kept it.

Pushing the cabinet door closed, locking it, and returning the keys to their drawer, she scanned the office, ensuring it was exactly as she'd found it.

"Beans?" she said, opening the envelope in her room. "What are these?" Several of the brain-looking beans knocked into pieces. "Why are they locked away in a folder?" Lifting them, she inhaled the faintest scent of something... earthy. She held them closer. The scent was not of these woods by her house, but one so faint, hidden beneath the scent of the cabinet, beneath the scent of papers and files, beneath the years in their envelope, a scent so untamed the only thing Ariel could think to do was eat it.

Her teeth shattered several of the nibs, grinding them to a pulp, yuck, it's like chalk. The chalk pasted up in the bathroom with a sip of water; swishing it out of her teeth, she drank it all.

With the envelope nestled securely beneath her pillow, she let herself surrender to the tide of exhaustion. Her eyes closed, her senses stretched outward, no longer tethered to the room around her. The bitterness in her mouth dissolved, threading into her bones. A vibration swam through her marrow, pulling her into the unseen world she often wrote about. Not violently, but like a feather alighting on a still pond, creating ripples that reached far beyond their origin. Like cacao that didn't know its role in the modern world, that didn't care if it was wrapped in Valentines, or the butt of a joke—the way the Land of Ought demanded its chocolates to be, buried under expectation. This was unyielding, alive.

The cacao lingered, spreading warmth from her chest outward, filling spaces she hadn't known were hollow. Then came the sound—a low, humming resonance deep within the trees, traveling up their branches and into the air, whispering an invitation.

An invitation to the Land of Ought Not.

Later that night, her hand found the envelope hiding beneath her pillow. And, she waited for the house to quiet. For her parents to finish reading. And for the click of their lights, signaling they'd gone to bed. Signaling her out of bed, where she moved with deliberate care. The crank handle of her window resisted slightly, turning slowly, pushing the glass open inviting in the chill of autumn. The air kissed her cheeks as she removed the screen. Beyond the edge of her room, the roof stretched like a small stage, and she stepped onto it, her bare feet adjusting to its cold shingled surface.

With practiced ease, she descended the ornamental cherry tree outside her window. Its gnarled branches, familiar from countless escapes to mail the Flower Lady letters, bowed slightly under her weight. Reaching the last branch, she hesitated, then jumped lightly to the ground. The landing was soft, her nightgown whispering against the dew-kissed grass. She froze, listening for any sound from her parents' room, but the house remained silent.

She slipped into the darkness, her form gliding across the field. The moonless night cloaked her, though her white nightgown flickered like a ghost's shimmer among the deep shadows of shrubbery and towering maples. If anyone had glanced out their window, they might have seen her—a fleeting figure moving purposefully toward the tree line.

The woods greeted her as she moved carefully over roots and uneven ground. Soon, she reached the special pine tree, its massive root jutting out of the earth like a gnarled elbow, weathered and ancient. Beside it stood the abandoned shack, its silhouette broken and sagging under the weight of time.

Ariel knelt beside the tree, the earth damp and cool beneath her. Her hands sank into the soil, tracing the shape of the buried glass jar. Beneath the weathered lid, she placed the envelope holding the mysterious contents. Little did she know what those beans were or that at that moment, thousands of miles away, deep within a tropical rainforest, the last of a small reminiscence of legend grew. Ariel stood, brushing her knees.

Unbeknownst to her, a confluence had been formed. Setting the seeds toward the chocolate syndicate.

Chapter Twelve

The rustle of paper filled the quiet kitchen. Ariel, now sixteen, flattened the business section of the newspaper on the table. A secret habit that had begun years earlier when her small fingers tracing the jagged patterns of the stock market charts. Numbers. Lines. A time when her teeth pressed into her lower lip and her pencil pressed onto the page.

When she'd write, "Dear Flower Lady," in careful, deliberate strokes. "Today we are going to discuss why money is important and look at why money can change people." and mail the letter in moist earth by the pine tree.

But now, the memory and the numbers meant nothing. The language was useless, a relic to a time that no longer existed. It wasn't the markets she was thinking about. Instead, she smoothed the edges of a crumpled letter in her hand and stepped outside. Her bare toes barely printing in the dry earth around the mailbox. This letter wasn't for the Flower Lady.

***

Life for Ariel vacillated between two extremes: survival and peace. Peace in the rare moments when she found time alone and survival was trying not to upset anyone when she wasn't.

At a national championship swim meet, walking along the cement seem on the sidewalk toward the natatorium, Ariel was finishing a chocolate éclair. Her steps were intentionally slow, avoiding one of her father's "no pressure" pep talks.

"Do you always walk the thin line?" A young man's voice asked playfully.

Looking over her shoulder a pair of bright eyes met her; Is he talking to me? "I like to practice walking straight."

"Oh. Sorry, I thought you were someone else." Then the voice chuckled, "Did you say you like to practice walking straight? Is that what you said?"

"Yes, so my feet don't turn in," stating what she thought was obvious.

His smile was contagious.

"Sometimes my feet turn in when I walk, and they shouldn't." Walk straight, walk straight. her father's cadence played in her mind. "I am training them. To walk straight I mean."

"Well, they are looking rather straight from here. What are you doing here, aside from the intense training?"

"I am swimming." Ariel did a quick survey of the area for any sign of her dad.

"You're swimming? You look pretty young!"

Ariel looked at him as if he'd fallen off a distant planet.

"Let me restate that, you look pretty but young. My name is David, what's yours?" He extended his hand to hers.

"I'm Ariel. And I just look young. I'm sixteen. What are you doing?" Ariel cautiously lifted her hand towards his. *Is this a joke?*

"I'm offering to shake your hand." Taking hers in his, "It's what people do when they meet each other."

She blushed, "I know that. I meant what are you doing here? Well not here holding my hand, but here in Arizona?" She shook her hand free. "Are you swimming too?"

"Sadly no, a shoulder injury so no swimming this year, just here supporting my teammates."

"Oh, I am sorry. I hope it gets better soon." Ariel scanned once again for her dad.

"It's starting to feel better now," rotating his shoulder, "maybe you're good luck."

Now I know he is not from Earth.

"Oh hey, there are my friends. I will see you later Ariel, good luck." Hopping the railing he landed between two of his classmates.

After Ariel's event that morning David startled her outside the locker room. "You've got a pretty nice stroke... for a midget."

She didn't say anything.

"Do you want to get lunch? My friends have ditched me to warm up. I have a few minutes to talk if you'd like."

Ariel nodded knowing her father was still on the pool deck watching her teammates.

"Boy you are quite a talkative young lady aren't you?" Hitting her with a little sarcasm.

She crossed her arms, "What would you like to talk about?"

"Nothing in particular. Why don't you ask me a question." He took the swim bag from her shoulder without thinking twice.

"Ok. How old are you?" She asked running her fingers along the seams in the cement wall as they walked towards the concession area.

"I am twenty. A Junior at Notre Dame."

"Oh. How come you're talking with me? Why do you want

to have lunch?"

"Because I usually find the most interesting people are those who walk the cracks in sidewalks. And second because I am hungry and thought you might be too. I have some peanut M&M's, do you want some?"

Her arms relaxed as she opened her hand. "Sure. I'd love some. Although... you are a stranger.... I'd better be careful."

He dropped one onto her palm and laughed. "Oh, she has a hidden sense of humor." Then he bought bagels and apples from the concession stand. "Where shall we eat our fine meal fit for champions?"

"By that tree, if you'd like?" She suggested. "And chocolate really is good luck. I've found when I eat a chocolate éclair before I swim, I get my best times." She stood taller.

"I just knew you liked it from the look in your eyes when you ate the M&M's, do you like peacocks?" David put the swim bag down and sat beneath a small oak tree, Ariel sat on the other side of the tree.

"That is a really weird question. But yes, I do. Why?"

"My mom told me they were good luck when I was young, and I've carried them with me ever since."

"That's really neat."

He reached around the tree and handed her one of the thin delicate feathers. "I am probably not going to see you too much this weekend. I will be hanging out with my friends from school. But maybe we could write to each other? May I have your address?"

"Like pen pals?" She wrote her address on a scrap of paper, a grin tugging at the corners of her lips. They would be messengers, trading parchment and secrets like travelers in some hidden realm. Her letters would ride on the wings of a snow-white dove, its feathers dusted with moonlight, soaring over mountains and seas to reach him. David's replies would arrive carried by a sleek black falcon, its piercing eyes holding the promise of faraway lands she could only imagine. She had other pen pals, but none like David. The others were approved by William—kids of people he knew.

Over the next year, their letters became more than words—they were the tether binding her earthbound life to something larger, something magical. She envisioned David's writing desk not as a simple piece of furniture, but as a great ancient table, set in a tower that overlooked an endless forests. His words, so carefully chosen, might have been spells, guiding her through his world of pre-medical studies and anatomy lectures. He described his studies with reverence. And, when he wrote about the girl at the library, one he wanted to ask to the symphony. Ariel imagined her laugh echoed like the song of soft wind chimes that brightened his days.

And Ariel, too, let herself write more openly. She shared fragments of her theories about how the world worked not just in reality but in the spaces behind it. She wondered aloud in her letters, and David didn't laugh at her musings. Instead, his replies came like lanterns in the dark, illuminating her imaginings with questions of his own, teasing out the edges of her ideas and letting them grow.

The dinner table was a war camp, though no one had declared it as such. Ariel's father sat like a brooding general, his sharp gaze an arrow searching for its mark. He didn't need to say anything; the anger radiated from him in waves, coiling through the air and settling on her shoulders. Ariel's fork clinked against her plate, an accidental strike of a sword against a shield, a sound too loud, too revealing. She had already lost.

The tension thickened. Her father rose abruptly, his movements harsh and methodical, like a hunter pouncing upon prey. A tight clench to the back of her neck and it is easier to control the claimed animal. Dragging Ariel to his bedroom and pinning her to the wall, he reached above the wardrobe, his hand moved to find its weapon.

Did air find its way into her lungs, she didn't know, her mind was retreating into safer spaces.

A letter. That is what his hand retrieved.

Her toes barely touched the carpet as her father turned slowly with the eyes of a dragon, breath hot with flames. The letter in his grip might as well have been her soul, torn from her and held aloft like a trophy. The air in the room grew thicker, darker, until Ariel felt herself slipping into the very edges.

"Dearest Ariel"—a growl replaced the reading.

It was a letter from David, now a senior at Notre Dame.

After school, before afternoon swim practice, and every Saturday, Ariel would position herself near the window in the front room, where the curtains hung like sentinels, guarding her watch. They had been able to stay in this house for almost a year now and the rhythm of the mail carrier's approach—the gravel crunching under tires, the hollow clang of the mailbox lid, the hum of the engine as it retreated down the lane, became routine. Each time, she would slip out before her father could notice, her fingers brushing the edge of the letters like a thief retrieving stolen treasure.

But on this particular Saturday, the ritual broke.

The day had been heavy, weighed down by clouds that clung to the sky. In the kitchen, quickly scrubbing a pan, Ariel tried to get to the mail on time while her father sat in the next room, his voice a low rumble on the phone. She hadn't heard the mail carrier come—perhaps the rain-softened earth had muffled his arrival, or perhaps the clatter of dishes drowned out the familiar sounds, perhaps he came early. But whichever it was, the floor fell from beneath her feet, the stack of mail already placed by her younger brother on the hall dresser.

She moved swiftly down hallway which stretched longer than usual. She casually shuffled the letters, tidying the magazines and other knickknacks around them.

"Ariel," her father stood in the doorway with her bother smiling beside him.

"I was just... tidying." she asked, trying not to sound expectant. "Anything good in the mail today?"

"Should there be?" he asked.

Her bother's cheshire smile grew with his ever so slight nod.

"Not really. I was just wondering."

But now, only a few hours later, a salty tear began slipping from the corner of her bulging eyes. He tightened his hold. Breath barely came.

Get it over with. Do it. Kill me. I dare you, Ariel thought loud and hard, challenging him silently. Then, realizing she didn't actually want her life to end at that moment, she changed her mind. *Never mind, I just want to go home! Please! Help me find home!* She prayed—to whom she didn't know, but she prayed just the same. Usually, the image of a twisting vine of cocoa pods showed up, or flying kites with her father.

It was just a letter, she thought. It was just a letter, a letter I shouldn't have gotten. A letter I didn't deserve from a friendship I didn't earn. It will not happen again. She saw David smiling behind her, handing her a delicate feather, an image of him writing letters. I am a fraud. He thinks I am a nice girl. What a shock it would be for him to see me like this, an unwanted Raggedy Ann. An image appeared of Raggedy Andy lifting Raggedy Ann from danger, only to drop her . . .

Raggedy Ann fell, lost in a dark corner.

Once the stars cleared from her vision, Ariel crawled back to her room. Face down on the carpet, each loop became a blade of grass. Sweet scents of morning dew rose, singing birds circling high above. Sun radiated upon her shoulders. Her early childhood swayed in the breeze. Reaching for her doll, Ariel brought Kitty to her chest for a few moments before getting up, setting Kitty on her bed, and turning to touch the door as if it were the old sycamore. She walked down the hallway into the dark forest where her dad sat on his throne. Her throat swelled with unwept tears.

"Yes, Ariel?" he asked.

The birds fell silent. The breeze stood still. A roll of clouds came in.

"I have something to say." She stood like a moss-covered stone.

The room shrank around them.

"The only reason I can say this is because I am not really your daughter, and you are not really my father." Her words were chosen to hurt. She wanted to hurt him, but even more than that, she wanted them to hurt herself. *But I've always wanted to be your real daughter. I'm sorry I said that, Dad.* She only thought that part though. William and Emily had never loved Ariel any less than if she had been naturally theirs. It was Ariel that had felt differently all along. Her younger siblings reminding her she was just a guest and not one of them.

His eyebrows signaled to go on. The protective scales around his heart had been hit; pain shone through the barriers he held close.

"This is not a family." She chose those words to hurt too. By this point in their lives, her father and mother had lost everything. Through her father's desperate attempt at existing—spending all their money on mistresses, cars, and vacations—ultimately, he had lost their house. Food on the table was no longer a guarantee but a daily gamble, and the roof over their heads had become a transient notion, traded between motels and cheap rentals, mail was forwarded like the wind to follow them. Ariel had learned to pack lightly, to fold her life into suitcases that were always one step away from being left on the curb. Stability had become as fragile as the plaster walls of the places they briefly called home, prone to cracking under the slightest pressure.

Her father carried himself like a man trying to hold back a dam, his shoulders perpetually flexed under the weight of something no one else could see. He had fought in Vietnam, though the word fought seemed too simple for what he had endured. Ariel knew it was not an absence of memory but a fortress of it. His trauma roared within, pounding ruthlessly against the barriers he had built to contain it. Those around him—neighbors, coworkers, even her mother—seemed to think they were helping by pretending the fortress didn't exist. Maybe they believed that by ignoring the waves of horror battering its walls, they were sparing him from reliving them.

At night, when the rest of the house was still, she would hear him. His muffled cries, his jagged breaths—it was like listening to someone drowning just beyond her reach. Once, she had crept to the living room in the middle of the night and found him there, crouching behind the couch with his head in his hands, trembling. His shadow against the wall looked monstrous, like the silhouette of a man and his ghosts tangled together, unable to separate. She hadn't dared speak, afraid that even the softest word might shatter him completely.

Then there were other times. Like the fireworks. It hadn't even been the Fourth of July. Some boys down the street had lit a string of firecrackers in broad daylight, their sharp cracks cutting through the quiet. William had dropped to the ground faster than Ariel thought possible, his hands flying over his head, his body curled into the hard earth of their yard.

In recent years, the cracks in his mind had spread outward, seeping into their family's life like water through a failing levee. They lived in hotels for stretches of time, only to come back to rental houses that never stayed theirs for long. Ariel had vivid memories of returning home one afternoon to find their belongings—suitcases, furniture, even the little knickknacks her mother cherished—piled unceremoniously on the sidewalk. A bright orange eviction notice had been taped to the door, flapping in the wind, mocking them.

Yet through it all, Ariel loved her father. She loved him with the fierce loyalty of a child who understood more than she let on. And William loved her too, in the quiet, solemn way of a man who had forgotten how to show love but never stopped feeling it. She saw it in the rare moments when his hand rested on her shoulder, a weight that carried both his affection and his apology. She saw it in the way he looked at her when he thought she wasn't paying attention, his eyes filled with a desperate kind of hope.

But love, Ariel had learned, wasn't always enough to hold back the long-reaching effects of something as vast and insidious as war. The scars left by events like Vietnam didn't heal cleanly. They hid deep, corroding even the bravest souls from within, until the pain seeped out like venom into the world around them. And while William tried to keep his pain buried, Ariel could feel it, creeping into their lives, reshaping them. Some days, it felt like they were drowning together, sinking slowly.

But, at this moment, as their world spun out of control, Ariel and her father resided in the storm's still eye. Tensions poised, the love buried deep between them wanted to say stop, but that love was intentionally pushed aside as pain surfaced.

"This is not how you treat your child—or any child for that matter," Ariel said. Her fingers fretted at her sides. "Do you know what it even means to love someone?" she asked and caught a flash of unfathomable sadness in his eyes. *I know you do. Remember it . . . Please, Dad. The first bite of chocolate. That was real. That was love. I want to go home. I want to go home with you. Please fly a kite with me. Hold my hand, Daddy. Please.*

"Are you done?" he asked, tucked behind an emotionless façade, and returned to the news.

A whirlpool whipped through the room. Cacao flew from her hand, crumbling into powder, landing in a faraway forest where on the ground it sprouted roots. "Find me!" it said just before the earth swallowed it, burying it out of sight.

***

Now, at just seventeen years old, while she and her mother were visiting Susan in Oregon, she tiptoed through the dune grasses — a blue seagull watching her. Thick mists were determined to wet the dark chestnut tresses edging her face. The ocean's tide rolled in wave after wave, a melody in the wind. Driftwood scattered the Oregon beach. There were no kites in the sky, but light streaked through the cloud layer over Proposal Rock, welcoming her invitation. To propose an idea, especially to Mother Nature herself, one mustn't ask in haste.

Ariel's chest expanded with a trill of electricity, and she closed her eyes. "I want to go home." She hugged her china doll that hid below the cables of her woolen sweater and stretched the neck open to kiss the delicate porcelain skin.

Life flew across her mind like a gull's wings working its way out of a storm, eventually freezing it in the space of cold sand and salty air. There wasn't much to propose. She hadn't much to offer besides the longing for impossibility. The blue gull landed by her feet, scratching at its down, waiting for the rock's response, and the mists grew to look more like rain.

"I want to go home," She cried silently. "How do I get there? Please help me."

Not long after, back in Southern California, Ariel began pulling things from the garage—boxes of tools, old furniture, odds and ends, things she believed her parents had forgotten they owned. The concrete floor was cold beneath her knees as she sifted through the remnants of their lives, her hands trembling as they touched items that hinted of a life so far removed from her now that maybe it had only been a dream. A wrench, rusted at the edges; a faded lampshade, frayed at its seams; a small ceramic owl with one cracked wing. She arranged them all on the driveway while the rest of her family was away at a swim meet for her younger siblings. She placed them all with the care of someone building an altar, though her offerings were to desperation, not gods.

She didn't want to leave. Every fiber of her being screamed to stay, to cling to the tattered edges of her world and hold them together with her bare hands if she had to. But the walls around her were crumbling, and she didn't know how to stop it. She didn't know what else to do. She thought of Susan, and Susan's escape.

Ariel was thirteen then, small and quiet, hiding from the storm that brewed in her house. It was just before her family moved to Southern California, From the upstairs window, she'd seen Susan standing in the driveway, her figure framed by the faint glow of the cloud-hidden moon. A soft mist dripped from the evening sky; it clung to everything and blurred the edges of the world. Susan's boyfriend, tall and lanky with an old bug car that coughed when it started, was at her side, his voice too low for Ariel to hear but his urgency unmistakable. He was trying to help her, trying to get her out.

Downstairs, the front door slammed open. William's voice tore through the air, louder than the mist, louder than the night. "Susan!" he barked, his figure looming as he marched toward the driveway. "Get back here."

Ariel pressed her forehead against the cold glass. She couldn't see Susan's face from where she stood, but she could feel her fear. William's wrath only reached Ariel and Susan; the other children had no idea what it was to be on the receiving end—William never touched them. Susan's fear radiated outward, and she tried to move away from William's approach. "No," Susan said, her voice carrying just enough for Ariel to hear through the window.

Susan tried to step toward her boyfriend's car, and he opened the passenger door, glancing nervously between Susan and the man who was now just feet away.

William's fist came out of nowhere. Ariel didn't see it land, but the sound of it—flesh against flesh, the sudden, sickening thud—made her jerk back from the window. Susan staggered, her hand flying to her face, and for a moment, Ariel thought Susan might fall. But she didn't. She stood there, shoulders trembling, even as William's voice thundered again. He grabbed her arm and brought her back into the house.

Susan's boyfriend drove off. Everything was still. The world was stuck in the dark hand of fate.

Minutes later a police car, followed by Susan's boyfriend, pulled up and two officers stepped out cautiously, their movements slow as they approached the house. William stepped outside, pacing, his anger radiating like heat. Susan's boyfriend stood a few feet away.

Ariel pressed her forehead to the glass again, holding her breath as she watched Susan walk out of the house. The officers turned to her, their voices calm, professional, as they asked her questions Ariel couldn't hear. William's voice rose again, sharp and angry, but this time the officers turned toward him, raising their hands to hold his rage at bay.

"Do you want to press charges?" one of the officers asked Susan, loud enough for Ariel to catch the words through the open window.

Susan shook her head. "No. I just want to leave," she said quietly, her voice steady despite the tears that streaked her face. "Can you stay here while I get my things?"

Ariel's throat tightened as she watched Susan walk back into the house one last time, her movements purposeful and unyielding. The officers flanked her, standing between her and William as she stepped inside. She returned minutes later with a small bag slung over her shoulder and climbed back into her boyfriend's car without another glance at the house.

The car pulled away slowly this time, no screeching tires, no rush.

Ariel had stayed at the window long after the taillights disappeared into the mist, the image of her sister's departure burned into her memory. That night, she had thought Susan was the bravest person she'd ever known. But now, as she turned back to the present, her own escape ahead of her, she wondered if Susan had felt as scared as she did now.

Each item she sold that afternoon felt like a small betrayal, like peeling away another layer of the life they had built, imperfect as it was. The neighbors had come and gone throughout the day, browsing her makeshift sale with casual interest, completely unaware of the weight of what they were buying. To them, it was a cheap hammer or an old rocking chair. To Ariel, it was survival—each dollar folded into her palm felt heavier than gold.

As the sun began to sink, its light turning the driveway to amber, she hesitated, the last few unsold items placed back in their spots just in time for her family to return. Her chest felt tight, her breathing shallow, and an overwhelming sense of wrongness settled over her. She stood there for a moment, staring at the door to the house, and then, before she could stop herself, she went inside.

Her mother's bedroom door was slightly ajar, and Ariel paused there, her hand resting on the frame. Inside, her mother sat on a small chair next to the bed, her body bent slightly forward, her hands clasped in her lap. The room was dim, the moonlight filtered through thin curtains, and it made her mother look smaller than Ariel remembered, her edges softened by shadow.

Ariel stepped into the room, the floor creaking under her weight. She didn't speak at first, didn't even know what she wanted to say. She only knew that part of her—a desperate, childlike part—hoped that her mother would look up, would see the turmoil in her eyes, would somehow know without being told what was about to happen. That she would stop Ariel, pull her into an embrace, and tell her that everything would be okay. Even if it was a lie.

But her mother didn't look up. Her gaze remained fixed on the floor, her thoughts distant. Ariel took a step closer, and then another, until she was standing right in front of her. She bent down slightly, wrapping her arms around her mother's shoulders, and hugged her tightly. She clung to her as though she might disappear if she let go, her own breath hitching in her chest.

"Mom," Ariel whispered, her voice barely audible. She wanted to say everything in that moment. But, Ariel saw the emotional pain her mother was in, William bullied her emotionally, he ignored her when he wasn't, she was tired. Ariel wished she could make it better, wished she could save her mom too. But the words lodged in her throat. Instead, she closed her eyes, willing her mother to sense it somehow, to feel what she couldn't say.

"I love you, Mom," she said finally, the words falling from her lips like the end of a prayer.

Her mother stirred slightly, lifting her head just enough to meet Ariel's gaze. There was warmth there, but also exhaustion, a deep weariness that seemed to stretch into that wordless void. "I love you too, Ariel," her mother replied softly, her voice like the faintest echo in a vast, empty room.

Ariel straightened, releasing her grip, though part of her didn't want to let go. She lingered for a moment longer, searching her mother's face for some sign—any sign—that she knew what was about to happen. But her mother didn't say anything, how could she have known? *I'm sorry, Mom. I'm so sorry,* Ariel's heart screamed at her, *"Ariel, do not do this. Do not leave."* Her mind answered back, *"I'm going."* as she turned and stepping back out of the room, out the front door into the amber light of the driveway. Walking away from the house, she had left something behind—a piece of herself. A piece that she would never quite get back.

***

Ariel's fingers trembled as she fumbled a quarter into the slot, but she never dialed. The phone's cold, plastic receiver hung limp in her grip, her thumb hovering over the buttons, tracing the numbers by heart.

She could still hear her mother's voice in her head. Ariel, honey, did you sleep well? Ariel, do you want tea? Ariel, be safe.

The air inside the phone booth was thick with the scent of rain and old paper. The glass walls were smeared with fingerprints, names scratched into the surface, the ghosts of people who had stood here before her. A car passed, its headlights flashing through the streaked panes, momentarily illuminating the storm of regret in her chest.

She pressed her forehead against the cool metal of the phone, her breath fogging the receiver. Go home. She could still turn back. Her mother might already be pacing, searching the house, calling her name. By now, she had probably checked the closets, the back porch, the laundry room, whispering, "Where is she?"

Ariel clenched her jaw and squeezed her eyes shut.

But going back meant more nights of staring at the ceiling, willing herself to disappear.

Her mother would cry. She could see it—Emily sitting on the edge of the bed, face buried in shaking hands, wondering what she did wrong. Wondering why Ariel didn't even say goodbye.

A sharp sob pressed against her ribs, but she swallowed it down. No. She couldn't think about that now.

She slid down until she was crouched on the floor of the

booth, knees pulled to her chest, the phone still cradled in her hands. The rain whispered against the metal frame, a soft, relentless tapping, like fingers against a locked door.

A decision had been made tonight. A door had closed.

And so she stayed in the phone booth, alone, watching the world blur behind sheets of rain.

Chapter Thirteen

"This is your captain speaking." The overhead voice jolted me back to the present. "We've had a change of course for a medical emergency."

Cabin lights dimmed, dissolving my dream into an illusionary mist. Damion sat up, scratching his head while Harvey rubbed his eyes, struggling to prop himself up on one elbow.

"We've diverted to Copenhagen Airport. Will be touching down in approximately twenty minutes."

"I hope whoever is sick is okay," I said, looking for Madge to inquire but not seeing her.

"Me too." Damion yawned, looking out the window. "Hey, while you were sleeping, I was thinking about the story. Can you tell me, did Ariel and Stuart remain friends?"

"They did," I said.

"I knew it!" Damion smirked. "And, you know, that story about Ariel burying the cocoa beans... it's kind of stuck with me." "Did she ever go back for them?"

A small, knowing smile creeped onto my face. "That's something we'll find out as the story goes along."

Damion lifts his hand in a quick, casual stop. "Good. Just keeping track, that's all." He takes a sip of his drink, his expression unreadable.

But as I watch him, a quiet unease stirs in my mind. Had I actually said she buried them? Or had I just thought it while dozing, lost in memory? I must have let it slip without realizing.

The plane touched down onto the wet tarmac. Madge eased the rheostat lighting up gradually so our eyes could avoid the shock of brightness as we pulled up to the gate.

"Wow, it seems even darker with the red lights blinking out there," Damion said, looking out his window again. "They're taking one of the pilots out on a gurney to the ambulance."

"Damion," I whispered, "see if Madge is around."

"I don't see her, but I'm monitoring Oceanic Center. Not only do we have a copilot with a heart attack or something, but on final approach they found a malfunction of the flight software. It has to be replaced."

"Well, I hope he will be okay." Emergency vehicles haunted

my thoughts. Lights blazed in the dark sky, an ominous feeling. Movements of police officers, firefighters, and paramedics seemed out of focus, removed. The weight of a man's body in my lap and the warmth of his blood seeping through my dress, then the thought tucked itself away as quickly as it came, once again behind the protective walls of my heart.

A flight attendant announced an extended layover, "If you'd like to grab your bags, we are disembarking the plane."

As we filed out, Melony sidled up to me.

"Do you think you could keep going with the story while we wait?"

"Yeah, I'm interested in hearing more too," Harvey said, catching up to us.

"Just a minute," interrupted Harvey. He put up both hands like a referee and leaned forward, lifting his hand and calling out, "Madge!" Then he sat back. "Listen, Madge, do you know how long we're gonna be stuck here?"

"We will get going as soon as we can. The crew was told at the latest tomorrow, if we need another plane."

"What's wrong with ours?" Harvey questioned.

Damion joined the chat. "They don't trust the guidance software. Something they detected on final approach. When we have a plane to safely fly us over the ocean, they will put us on it."

"Jesus, can't they pilot a plane? Hell, the Wright brothers didn't need software."

"Harvey, dear man," said Madge, "the Wright brothers weren't responsible for so many passengers. I'll go see what I can find out."

"Oh! I have a joke about the Wright brothers," said Melony, rubbing rose-scented lotion into her hands. "Okay here goes, are you ready?" We nodded. "Do you know what Wilbur told Orville when their plane first took flight? What he was yelling while running down the hill after the plane?"

Harvey shouted the punch line, "Orville, I told you that thing wouldn't hold the road!" He pushed his sliding glasses back up the bridge of his nose to the sound of ersatz laughter. "So where is all of this going? We've got mysterious beans that no one can find, and we've got an adoption and the backstory. Obviously, it's all going to come together, but when?"

Damion chimed in with a question too: "Not to jump around so much, but I was just wondering, did Mary ever come back? What happened to her? Did she and Ariel ever meet? Did she have any more children? And... where is the cacao plantation?"

"Mary didn't have any other children. And Harvey, yes, it is all coming together very soon." I watched him try to get comfortable in his seat with his legs extended like a ski slope in front of him and his hands folded into a pout.

"I need to ask again. I know you told us before; you said Ariel had kids. How many?" Harvey asked.

"Three children. All boys. The youngest, Brandon, is about your age, thirty-three." I turned and nodded again at Damion, "David is her oldest, he'd've been about thirty-nine, and Gresham is about eighteen months behind David at thirty-eight."

Melony shuffled from one side to another, readjusting her bags and making them into a pillow-like backrest, and asked, "So if I were to guess, Stuart had something to do with the children? You kind of sped through that part."

I nodded. "You are correct, but Ariel and Stuart never married. Brandon's father had always been Ariel's friend. He was a dear friend who helped ... What's the best way to describe this ... Like Gresham, Brandon was by design."

Harvey, unbashful, shared his opinion. "She's not particularly good keepin' men around. Some women are just too ... too easy."

The eyes of all the women in our small group widened at Harvey's comment, and I said, "Harvey, a few things: Have you ever been with more than one woman?" He didn't respond—not verbally, anyway. "Not everyone is meant for marriage. Ariel knew this about herself. Plus, she remained good friends with both Stuart and Brandon's dad. And she wanted a family more than anything. And lastly, not that it is relevant to the story, she decided celibacy was her path in life."

Madge came back with an update. "It looks like our layover will be on the longer side. We are waiting for a new flight crew and a new plane."

"How is the copilot?" Damion inquired returning to our group after buying everyone cold drinks.

"He should be fine. Like I said, we are waiting for his replacement and have a new plane getting ready."

"That's a relief," Melony sighed. "Can you join us? Or do you have to go with the rest of the crew?"

"I can stay." Madge smiled. "I've got my phone." She moved to sit near Damion. "So, what about you? What's your family like?"

Damion, mid-sip of his drink, lowered his glass slightly. "Oh, uh... not much to tell, really. Just me and my sister growing up."

Madge's eyes twinkled. "Older or younger?"

"Younger," Damion replied, swirling the ice in his glass. "By two years."

"And what does she do?"

A barely perceptible pause. Just a flicker—half a second

too long before he answers. "She's... in business." His voice was even, but the words were carefully chosen.

"Business? What kind of business?"

Damion shrugs, casual, but the way he shifts in his seat betrays something underneath. "Imports, mostly. Logistics, supply chain stuff. She's always been ambitious."

"You two close?" Madge asks.

Another pause. Just as subtle as the first.

"Not really." His brow raised. "Different paths, you know how it is."

For just a moment, he was somewhere else entirely.

"So, what happened between Ariel and Stuart?" Harvey led our attentions back to the story.

"They continued working. They were not always paired together, but they entered territory that could freeze your spine. In regard to the man from earlier, who shoved Ariel into his car, she did see him again—Ariel was working out of Houston, TX at this time. It wasn't a chocolate story, but its bitterness had its own taste.."

***

Peter had prepared her, given her the assignment, and there she was driving as rain stitched a fine lattice across the windshield, drops of quicksilver. Beside her, on the passenger seat, a leather folio held the life she wore today: ANNA KESSLER, Data Security Liaison, contract term ninety days, provisional clearance Level B.

Chapter Fourteen

The campus rose beyond the security lane like a clean geometry drawn against the night—glass, steel, the hush of engineered air. On the mirrored facade, the blue letters of Horizon BioSystems hovered with corporate assurance, not bright, exactly, but unblinking. Ariel let one breath anchor inside her ribs, then another.

The guard under the rain hood looked no older than twenty-two, cheeks raw from weather and caffeine. He leaned to the open window.

"Badge, please."

She offered it through the wave of rain. He scanned the plastic with a handheld wand that murmured green as it read who she was for the next few months, Anna Kessler.

The gate lifted. She set the car in motion; tires whispering over the wet asphalt.

Inside, the foyer was an atrium of glass and white stone, and was the kind of clean that pushes noise into the corners. An installation hung above the security desk: a helix of brushed steel rotating so slowly you could mistake its motion for a trick of peripheral vision. A receptionist offered a discreet nod, then studied her monitor; the printer behind her murmured a thin sheet of paper into the tray like a mechanical swallow.

"Ms. Kessler?" she said. "Dr. Patel will be right down."

For the next few months, she quietly followed rabbit holes, her gaze half on the numbers, half on the slender wires that ran behind the walls. She found documents, listened intently to any hush of conversation, pieced vocabulary to puzzles, and uncovered a picture.

Weights, dates, destinations. A remnant of a memo:

Bio-Asset Transfer Oversight: Division HL—21 // Basel Coordination

The Basel shone up at her with the softness of a streetlamp in fog.

She copied, printed and placed what she could into the folio beneath the leather, unseen.

Before leaving she glanced at a list of vendors that laid like a deck of passports on a table in Dr. Patel's office on her last day. Her brain photographing names from half a dozen cities, the same three dispatch numbers repeating like drumbeats under different coats.

She wrote three digits on a Post-it, nothing else, then unpeeled it. Fold once. Fold again. She slid it into her pocket, like a gum wrapper.

In the atrium, the helix rotated another invisible degree.

Once in her car, the folio lay on the passenger seat, patient. She drove. Not directly home, but stopped in a resident spot at an apartment community. Checked for any headlights or car than may have also pulled in. When none showed up, she opened folio, took the hidden pages, and read again—HL—21 // Basel Coordination—as if names could attest to themselves. She took a pen from the console, the kind designed to masquerade as something more: matte black, a little heavy, cap threaded. Unscrewing it released the small click of the hidden drive against metal. She touched it with a finger; the coolness threaded up her skin.

Unfold once. Unfold again. She copied the three digits from the Post-it to the back of the paper in pencil so soft it would vanish if someone rubbed it with a breath. The Post-it met its demise.

Returning to the road in silence to go home, a memory obliged: a child at the roots of a giant pine, a jar, a letter, a question addressed to the Flower Lady. She had another question now, grown tall enough to look back.

At home, heat ticked in the pipes, wind brushed the eaves, and the lake beyond the trees murmured in its sleep.

Ariel moved on socked feet through the hallway, carrying the faint light of a candle in a chipped glass. The scent of soap and damp juniper clung to her sleeves; the smell always reminded her of the boys after bath time.

David's door was half open. She leaned against the frame for a moment, watching the slow rise of his blanket. His lashes trembled with dreams, a cowlick lifting at the back of his head like a question mark.

He was six now—taller, surer—but when he slept she still saw the baby who used to curl his hand around her finger, who slept of her chest while she read.

She bent to adjust the quilt.

"Sweet dreams, Davie Boy," she whispered. "I love you." He murmured something about a Lego building he'd made, and her chest warmed with an ache that felt like both pride and apology.

In the next room, Gresham had kicked free of his covers again.

At five he was all motion, a creature of sunlight and scraped knees. She tucked him back in, smoothed the hair from his forehead, and kissed his cheek.

He sighed once and turned his face toward the window.

For a moment she simply stood between the rooms, candlelight trembling across the hall. After assignments she was given months off, and looked forward to that time with her children more than any other.

In her own room, she set the candle beside the window, turned on a small lamp and opened her notebook.

She wrote three words at the top of a clean page:

Follow the anomaly.

Then she looked once more toward the boys' rooms and added another line, softer, meant only for herself:

Keep them safe.

***

Ariel set the folio on Peter's desk. He closed his laptop and waited.

"You were inside Horizon longer than you were supposed to," he said.

"I had to be certain," she replied. "And now I wish I wasn't."

He motioned for the report. She opened the folder and slid the top sheet forward.

"Three cryo cycles each day, identical timing. The logs call them developmental sequencing. The materials are marked as donor substrates, but the metadata shows multiple age bands—infant through adult. Provenance fields are empty. Someone has rewritten the identifiers."

Peter studied the numbers as if they might reorder themselves. "Retention?"

"Extended beyond ethics by months. It's not research anymore—it's procurement."

He shut the folder gently. "Who's running the lab?"

"Patel's name is on the paperwork, but there's someone else behind her. A consultant—Lucia Veran. The files list her as a hematology adviser brought in for cross-disciplinary trials. I never met her, only heard her voice once in the corridor." Ariel's tone sharpened slightly. "She knows exactly what she's doing."

Peter leaned back. "Veran. I'll have Intelligence check her history."

"She'll have cleaned it. People like her always do." She hesitated, "Do you remember the man—the one who tried to force me into his car in San Diego? I saw him this week. Talking with Patel. I didn't stay long enough for him to notice."

His eyes lifted. "You're off the assignment as of tonight. No argument."

"Yes, I am. I encrypted the evidence and sent it to your secure node. May you please delete my local credentials right away."

He gave a short nod. "Done."

She turned toward the door, then paused. "One more thing. At the coffee shop near the Energy Corridor. A couple people were talking. It sounded like they're falsifying earnings through loans, using offshore shells, and they mentioned building a market to trade weather. I mean, they did not come out and say it directly, but..." She let the absurdity of it lighten her tone. "Then they drifted into tech. Said the future's streaming films instead of mailing DVDs, and picture frames that show digital albums. I told them the internet will need ratings like movies if that happens."

Peter gave a low chuckle. "You missed your calling. You should've gone to Wall Street—or joined the dot-com circus."

"Quantum physics seemed safer," she said. "At least until now."

He smiled, thin but real. "Safer doesn't mean quiet."

She reached for the handle. "Thanks again for the tip on the tech fund. Tight budget back then, but Qualcomm's doing just fine."

"Remind me to have you pick our next investment."

***

"Well, the same man who warned her being in the building talking to that doctor, I bet that was unnerving. Was she right about what she overheard in the coffee shop?" Melony asked while arranging the contents of her bag to soften it to use as a pillow. "And, what about the beans you told us about, the ones she ate as a child? Does she know those were the beans she was looking for? Does she find out? Are they part of the sabbatical?"

Before I could answer, Madge asked solemnly. "Did she die? Or, or, did he Stuart? You said earlier she loved him 'til the end."

"So much has happened, and so much is about to happen. Melony, she was on to something back then about the financial stuff in Houston, but let's save that for another time."

"I really don't mean to dig, but do you know where the cocoa beans are? Even just a hint?" Damion asked.

Air fill our space with the hum of the airport stretching—the tide of strangers moving past, the scent of coffee and perfumes.

Instead of answering Damion, I asked, "Have you ever felt the collision of choices? Like, you know, right after a choice is made, something is going to happen. But the feeling is so fast it's like a flash of spider lightning, or like when something dips so quickly under you, it leaves your stomach behind . . . that momentary hollow that causes a brief, unexpected panic." I thought about where our story is heading and decided where to tell it from here. "The day Ariel decided to begin the chocolate sabbatical, she had been thinking of her older sister," I explained. "She'd been thinking of the last time they were together."

* * *

2003

Susan's house was quiet when Ariel and her young boys arrived; the air was fragile, splintering with even the faintest sound. Susan was sitting propped up in bed, her skin pale, her breath coming slow and shallow. Her daughter, a lively six-year-old, sat cross-legged on the floor, humming softly as she colored. Ariel paused in the doorway; the sight of her sister, the outline of her body swallowed by the bed and layers of blankets.

Susan turned her head slowly, her lips curving into a faint smile when she saw Ariel. "You came," she said, her voice a raspy whisper.

"Of course I did," Ariel replied, stepping into the room. She knelt beside the bed, reaching for her sister's hand. Cold. Frail.

"I need a favor," Susan said, her tone soft but deliberate. She nodded toward her six-year old daughter, who had now turned her curious gaze toward the two of them. "Take her to the school fair for me. I promised her we'd go, but . . ." She let the words trail off, her eyes glancing down at her still body.

Ariel hesitated for a moment, then squeezed her sister's hand. "I'll take her," she said, her voice steady. "And we'll bring you back something special."

Susan let her head rest against the pillow. "Thank you," she murmured. Her daughter's face lit up, and Ariel felt a pang of bittersweet joy as the girl ran to her, grabbing her hand and pulling her toward the door with all the enthusiasm only a child could muster.

Ariel's sons stayed behind with her mother, who had just made tulip-shaped cookies for them to frost.

At the school fair, Ariel wandered through the bright stalls, her niece holding her hand, more interested in showing Ariel her classroom and artwork than playing at the booths. They meandered through the playground and stopped by the bake sale, picking out cookies and cupcakes wrapped in crinkling plastic. At the craft table, her niece insisted on selecting coloring books—one for her and one for her mother. "Me and my mom color together," the girl declared with absolute certainty, her little fingers tracing the outlines of the pages.

When they returned, Susan was awake, and her eyes brightened at the sight of her daughter, who ran to her bedside with the coloring books in hand. "Look, Mommy! We got you one, too!" she said, holding it up proudly.

"Thank you, sweetheart," she said, her voice barely above a whisper. Ariel placed the bag of treats on the bedside table, arranging it carefully so Susan could reach it. Her sister glanced up at her, and for a moment, their eyes met.

"Thank you," Susan said again, this time to Ariel. Her daughter climbed onto the bed beside her, snuggling close, and Susan wrapped an arm around her as best she could.

* * *

"I want chocolate," Susan whispered the next morning.

Lilacs bloomed beneath the window, their purple hearts spilling life into the air, a stark contrast to the stillness inside. . Ariel turned from the sill.

"Chocolate?" Ariel echoed, "I always remembered you as a vanilla girl." Crossing the room, she carefully brushed a strand of bangs from Susan's forehead.

"Your special chocolate," Susan said quietly. "The one from childhood. That's the one I want."

Ariel's chest tightened beneath an ache burning through her ribs. "That was a fairy tale, Susan. Just a dream." Her words faltered, heavy with the fear she'd disappoint again—always the wrong story, always the wrong sister.

"It's what I need now. I need a dream." Susan's voice was soft and heavy. "At least . . . tell me the story . . . once more." A shadow crossed her face, a question teetering on the edge of her lips. She swallowed, then pressed on, her tone firming despite its frailty. "I would never wish cancer on anyone. I thought you cursed me. You were always different. How did you know I'd get cancer?" Susan asked.

Silent tears stung Ariel's eyes, spilling over before she could blink them back. "I'm sorry, Susan," she whispered, her voice cracking under the weight of a memory that had divided them until now. "I'm so sorry." Ariel sank onto the bed's edge, her hands trembling in her lap, desperate to erase the echo of a curse she'd never meant to cast.

* * *

1982

"Here, Susan!" A molten mass of chocolate clung to Ariel's small hand. "Make a wish and taste this. It's better than a magic genie!"

"Ariel, I'm busy. I don't have time for these games."

"Just make a wish, Susan. You never know, it could really work!"

"Not now, Ariel." Susan's voice was firm. "Go do something else."

"Okay. Is that your wish?"

"Yes," Susan replied, "leave me alone."

Scraping her chocolate-covered palm against her teeth, Ariel spun around on socked feet, exiting the room while saying, "See, Susan, it worked. Your wish came true. I'm leaving."

They were young; Susan was just sixteen, and Ariel was eleven.

Susan used to always pay Ariel twenty-five cents for back rubs. One particular day, the energy Ariel felt from touching Susan was different. It disconcerted her.

"Do you feel okay, Susan?" she asked

"Yeah. Why?" Susan responded.

"You feel different. It's hot right here," Ariel said, pinpointing the small region so Susan could feel it.

"It's because I'm lying next to the fire," Susan said.

Ariel ruminated on the change in her sister's energy for weeks until the answer showed up one evening in her sleep.

The next morning, while Susan was in the shower, Ariel opened the bathroom door, steam slamming into her like a sauna. "Susan," she said.

The shower door opened, and Susan peaked out. "Yes?" Her

hair was sudsy with a concoction of beer and mayonnaise in an attempt to get rid of the chlorine burn from swimming.

"You're going to die of cancer." Her words were matter-of-fact.

Susan's eyes grew like saucers. "Why would you say that?" She opened the shower door wider with fear and anger. "Get out! Don't ever talk to me again!"

"I just wanted to help... I don't want you to die." The last words just flopped to the floor like a fish out of breath.

* * *

When the memory faded, Ariel looked to Susan. "How about I tell you the story of the Flower Lady?" she suggested.

Susan's eyes drew peaceful, "That would be nice," then gave way to slumber. Ariel once again tenderly brushed Susan's brow, and the story stayed in the clouds with the quietly whispering lilacs.

Delicate, Susan's hand was cool in Ariel's as she knelt on the floor. "Please, God, whomever you may be, please take care of her."

* * *

We sat for a moment while passengers from other flights moved between gates. Who knows where all our thoughts had gone before Madge took a breath. "Wow. I don't know what to say. I lost my mother to cancer, and it was horrible. I was really young, and it stayed with me all my life. I was seven. I was napping beside her. She was in hospice, and no one really told me what was going on. She died beside me. I didn't know she was dying; it was so scary. Her eyes just stared toward the window, empty, but there was no more pain. Her hand was still resting on me. I'll never forget. Then, after I went to get my dad, everything was a blur."

Damion took Madge's hand in both of his. "I'm so sorry," he said.

Madge nodded. "I don't tell that story to many people."

Damion rubbed her hand softly. "I'm glad you did."

Harvey, having enough of the emotional interaction, humphed and said, "So, what's next?"

Melony interjected to help smooth the transition, "I can see why that scene with Susan had such an impact on Ariel's decision. And I agree with Harvey, what happened next?"

"Well, Ariel stayed beside her sister for a few moments, her head bowed as though in prayer, before slowly rising to her feet. But when turned to leave, but her path was blocked by her younger brother who'd had just arrived. His arms crossed, his expression hard. She had known this moment might come—should have expected it, even—but it still hit her like a blow to the gut.

'What are you doing here?' he asked in a low, authoritative voice. He stepped closer, his eyes narrowing. 'You've got no right to be here...'

Ariel blinked, caught off guard. "Susan asked me to come," she said quietly, trying to keep her voice steady. "She wanted me here."

"Susan didn't know what she was asking," he snapped. Before she could reply, he grabbed her arm, his grip tight and unyielding. "You don't belong here. How stupid can one person be?"

He pulled her toward the door, his strength more than enough to force her along. Ariel stumbled, trying to keep her footing, her mind racing.

"Stop," she said, her voice shaking. "Please."

But her brother wasn't listening. He dragged her into the hallway, his words cutting through her like jagged glass. "You're not part of this family. You've never been part of this family. You think you can just show up, like you belong here, like you matter? You don't. You never did. Now, get your kids," he barked, his voice echoing down the hall. "They're not welcome either."

"She invited me." Ariel's voice quite like a child's trying to explain. Her chest tightened as she saw her children peeking around the corner, their wide eyes filled with confusion and fear. Her oldest, David, only ten, stepped forward hesitantly, his small hands balled into nervous fists at his sides.

"Mom?" he said softly, his voice trembling.

Ariel forced herself to stay calm, to keep her voice steady for their sake. "It's okay," she said, though her words felt hollow. "Come on, it's time for us to go; the others want to be with Susan now too."

Ariel's brother's lip curled with disdain as he stepped aside, giving them just enough room to pass. Ariel gathered her children, lifting her youngest, Brandon, as they made their way to the door. She could feel her brother's gaze on her back, could hear his muttered words as they left.

"You ruined this family, I wish they never adopted you," he said again, quieter this time but no less cutting. "Leave."

Ariel stepped outside; she didn't look back.

As she buckled her youngest into his car seat, she paused for a moment, resting her forehead against the doorframe. Tears pricked her eyes, but she refused to let them fall.

"I'm sorry," she whispered, though she wasn't sure if the words were meant for her children, for Susan, for her parents, or maybe for them all.

***

2010

The window latch stuck as Ariel pushed it open. Late summer air, thick with the hush of crickets, slipped into the kitchen, nudging the curtains. Somewhere beyond the trees, the river whispered over stone.

Her notebook lay open on the counter—half a page of notes scratched in ink, then nothing. Blank space waiting for answers that wouldn't come. She rubbed the heel of her hand against her temple and glanced at the clock. 9:12 p.m. David should've been home by now.

The hum of tires over gravel cut through the stillness. She left the kitchen, bare feet soft against the wood floor. The screen door creaked as she stepped outside.

David's car pulled up near the porch, engine clicking as it cooled. His silhouette moved through the half-light—broader now. Ariel saw the young man he'd become in the set of his jaw when he turned toward her.

"Hey," she called, stepping down from the porch.

"Hey, Mom. Sorry I'm late. Just saying goodbye to everyone before we scatter into the world."

She hugged him. "It's flown by. Silly as it sounds, I thought we'd have all the time in the world."

"I wouldn't trade it, though." He shifted the camera bag on his shoulder, gaze flicking toward the house—measuring the distance between past and future.

A shift of wind stirred the leaves overhead. Ariel swallowed against the tightness in her throat. "Come on, I'll make us some tea. Stuart called."

"What'd he say?"

Inside, Ariel lit the burner with a sharp click. The faint hiss of gas, the flick of flame.

"He wants to meet you for lunch when you get back from hiking and wants me to help him with a few jobs."

David pulled out a chair at the table. "Going back to investigations? That could be good." He noticed her glance at a cocoa pod on the shelf. "Doesn't mean you have to give up the research—just clear your mind a bit."

"Maybe."

"You've been chasing that cacao longer than I can remember," he said. "Not that we minded. We've had good life, a bit of a fairytale really. But maybe it's time."

She didn't answer. The kettle rumbled, heat building beneath its steel shell. Ariel gripped the edge of the counter.

"College, an Army Ranger, and Gresham heading off next

year," she said quietly. "It's been so neat watching you boys grow up. More than I ever dreamed." She turned to look at him. "And you're right—maybe a change is in order."

David set out two mugs on the rustic island he'd built the previous year. "Yep. You're not gonna find it by staring at old notes," he teased gently. "If you're stuck, shift the perspective. That's what you taught me."

Ariel leaned back against the counter. His eyes—so much like hers—held none of the boyish hesitation she remembered. He was already half in a world she couldn't follow.

The kettle hissed. Ariel reached to turn off the flame but paused, her hand hovering above the knob. "You know," she said softly, "part of me's afraid. Afraid to say goodbye." A few tears escaped, she thanked stars for sharing David.

"I'm heading out early. Thought I'd drive up to the ridge—watch the sunrise. Want to come?"

She nodded, words too heavy to shape.

He paused in the doorway. "Think about it, Mom. Maybe it's not about what you're looking for—maybe it's about why. Sweet dreams. I Love you."

"Goodnight, sweetheart. I love you too."

The screen door creaked open, then shut with a finality that caught in her chest.

***

2011

Ariel marked the same line in her notebook for the third time, the ink pooling slightly where her pen had paused too long. The kitchen window stood open, letting in the faint, mineral smell of dew clinging to the grass.

Footsteps shuffled down the hall. David home visiting, appeared, rubbing sleep from his eyes, hair still mussed from his pillow. The faint scent of wood smoke clung to his hoodie.

"Morning," he said, voice rough with sleep.

"Morning. Bonfire good?"

"Yeah, it was great." He grabbed the milk from the fridge and poured it into his granola bowl.

"You guys packed?" she asked instead.

"Mostly. Gresham's still stuffing things into his pack like we're leaving for the Yukon."

The phone rang. Before Ariel could move, Gresham's footsteps pounded through the hallway.

"Got it!" He snatched the receiver off the wall, breathless from the dash. "Hello?" A grin tugged at his mouth. "Hey, Stuart! ... She's fake reading," Gresham said, throwing Ariel a glance full of mischief.

"Nice," Stuart's voice crackled faintly through the receiver. "So, what's the plan before college?"

"Camping trip with David and Brandon," Gresham said, winding the phone cord around his wrist. "Then I'm driving out to school."

"Still undecided on a major?"

"Yeah, but probably something between biology, law, or maybe art history. I dunno. Guess I'll figure it out as I go."

"You've got time," Stuart said. A pause. "Hey, pass the phone to your mom, would you?"

Gresham covered the receiver. "He wants you."

David swung his hiking pack over one shoulder. "Mom, we're heading out."

"Hey. Wait. Stuart, let me call you back." She put the phone down and followed the boys to the porch. Brandon skidded into view, half-hopping as he crammed his foot into a sneaker.

"Stay sharp out there," she said. "Call if you need anything."

David pressed a kiss to her temple. "We've got it, Mom."

Gravel crunched beneath tires as the car rolled away part of her clung to the backseat.

"Hey," Stuart answered on the second ring.

"What's up?" Ariel asked.

"I've got a question and some news."

"Ok, News first, question second."

"You should sit down for this one."

"Just say it, Stuart."

"I'm getting married."

Ariel's pulse hitched. She clutched the receiver tighter, the plastic warm against her palm. "You're what?"

"Getting married. I wanted you to hear it from me first."

For a moment, the kitchen seemed to tilt, the floorboards had shifted beneath her feet.

"Wow," she said, forcing air through her lungs. "That's... unexpected. Congratulations."

"We're eloping."

"Eloping?" She traced a finger along the edge of her notebook. "Daring."

"Almost as wild as taking your lunch break five minutes early."

She huffed a laugh, though her chest still felt tight.

"How are you doing?" Stuart asked, his voice dipping into

something more serious.

"I'm ok. What's the real reason you're calling?"

"How about coming back to work? Can you head out here tomorrow?

"Possibly. The boys are camping for a week. What's going on?"

"Check your work mail."

"Ok, let me look. Hold on."

The briefing he emailed came through encrypted channels.

Subject: Briefing on Red Genesis–Zurich Assignment

Ariel,

Hope you're doing well. I know you weren't planning to dive back in yet, but this one needs your attention.

There's a biotech initiative called Red Genesis that's raising flags. A synthetic blood additive—Crimson Phase—designed to neutralize pathogens, but with the potential to be weaponized into something lethal.

The Clymenos Group is at the heart of it. Think tank, military contractors, pharma ties—the usual web. They're hosting a recruitment event at a conference in Zurich in a few days. We need to know who's involved, who's complicit, and most importantly, if this project is what we suspect it is.

Do you remember the name Dr. Lucia Veran?

Call me when you get this.

— Stuart

Somewhere outside, a crow called once, sharp and clear, Stuart's voice followed.

"I'll have you on the redeye, tonight."

"Let me think about it for a second. Logistically."

"Don't think too long," Stuart replied.

"Ok, I can be at Sea-Tac by 7:00-7:30. Let me call the boys quick before they are out of service and let them know the plan."

"Good." Stuart stated before the line went dead.

Chapter Fifteen

Madge and Damion seemed more comfortable around each other. The initial curious uncertainty between them on this journey had all gone away. Seeing her there, in her early thirties, with long blonde hair pulled back, she no longer looked the mothering image she had portrayed at the beginning of the flight.

Melony meekly raised her hand. "Could you tell me how that Greg fellow you mentioned comes into the story?"

"Good question, because that's exactly where we are," I said.

* * *

Ariel and Stuart sat in a small room, going over a project they were calling Red Genesis.

"Red Genesis," the presenter said, "is a multinational biotech initiative regarding biological weapons research." He paused, glancing at both of them. "Privately, the person hiring us believes it's a pretext for something far more offensive.

"The project's centerpiece," the presenter continued, "is something called Crimson Phase. It's a synthetic blood additive designed to bond with red blood cells and neutralize blood-borne pathogens—essentially acting as a biological shield. But there's more to it. When combined with a secondary agent, the additive can induce rapid clotting, catastrophic organ failure, or worse. Essentially, it can be weaponized."

"Of course it can," Stuart muttered under his breath.

"The project is remotely connected to the Clymenos Group, with ties to private research – just imagine for example Bill Gates' interest in vaccine development. Or a pandemic outbreak with a vaccine on hand ready to go."

"You mean create the problem which would allow using people as test subjects or worse. This makes me sick. Who knows what could be inside this." Ariel cut in. "They already poison our food supplies."

"They've been recruiting some of the world's brightest minds in hematology and bioengineering under the pretense of preventing biological warfare."

The next slide displayed a glossy promotional image for a biotech conference in Zurich. "Clymenos is hosting a recruitment event at this conference. We have reason to believe they're scouting. The presenter hesitated, his gaze flicking to the file. "We have intelligence that suggests their bioweapon—nicknamed Hemlock—targets specific genetic markers. They're working on a pathogen capable of targeting individuals or populations with precision."

After the presentation, the flight to Zurich felt endless. "You know," Stuart said, "I had a look at Veran's history."

"I remember her," Ariel said. "Her name came up in some case files years ago. That was a long time ago, around the time you and I met."

* * *

The conference was filled with scientists and biotech executives milling about in the expansive hall. Ariel and Stuart moved through the crowd like shadows.

Ariel's gaze settled on Dr. Veran, who works for Clymenos, standing near a booth, deep in conversation with a man.

She nudged Stuart.

"Dr. Veran?" Ariel said walking up to them.

Veran turned. "Yes?"

"I've followed your work for years," Ariel said, smiling with earnest. "I'd love to hear more about what you're working on now-a-days."

"I'm sorry," Dr. Veran said. "Who did you say you were with?"

"Rowland Institute," Ariel said using her alias. "Our research overlaps in a few areas—gene therapies, mRNA research, hematologic disorders. I've been following work on contagion countermeasures. It's really interesting."

Veran's eyes narrowed ever so slightly, her posture shifted. "Interesting," she said slowly. "Not many people share much about their work in that area. It must be quite the challenge keeping up with the rumors."

"It's not easy," Ariel admitted with a smile. "You're right, it is mostly rumors, but they're still interesting because I try to piece them together with published papers and articles."

"I'm afraid I can't comment on that," Veran said flatly. "You understand."

Veran moved away quickly just as Ariel's phone began to pulse with a message from Stuart: Meet me near the garden terrace.

"What is this?" Ariel asked, looking at a note he handed her.

"Names," Stuart said. "Veran's name is there, obviously. But so is someone else—Greg Denslock."

Ariel blinked. "Denslock." She thought for a second. " I think he's the oncologist, remember, that consulted for some medical analytics company… isn't he?"

"That's him," Stuart confirmed. "There's also Michael Roarke. And Veronica Cho, a bioethicist who's been consulting for Clymenos. I think these are people we can start with, we just want to meet them before handing over their names to see if they've been approached or what."

"Alright, I think we need to do this more casually." Ariel said, her mind already calculating how to approach this. "If they think we're digging for information, they might just hang up."

"Exactly," Stuart said. "Let's approach them casually. Learn who they are, what motivates them—then we will hand what we learn over and be on our way. This isn't anything I want to get tangled up in."

Ariel nodded, folding the list and tucking it into her pocket. "I'll reach out to half and you take the other. After this, I think I am really going to retire. I am tired of learning about all the underground darkness and feeling like there is nothing I can do."

"Ariel," Stuart placed his hands on her shoulders, "You are doing something, we are. We are doing what we can."

"One day, people are going to see all this for themselves, they are. And I don't think it is too far off because it is all starting to rumble close to the surface now."

Chapter Sixteen

After beginning initial contact with Michael and Veronica, Ariel moved on to Greg.

It was lunchtime in Florida.

"Hi, may I speak with Greg . . ." Ariel said, tapping her forehead, knowing she should've asked for him using his last name.

"Greg who? Oh, you the mean the doctor?" the receptionist asked.

"Yeah, I had a question and was hoping he might have a minute to talk." Ariel scribbled circles on the notepad in front of her.

"Well, he's at the hospital right now. Can I take a message?"

"No, that's okay. Is there a better time to call?" Ariel asked.

"He's pretty busy, but leave your name, and he'll get back to you." The receptionist was already tired of the back and forth.

"No. Thanks anyway," Ariel said before hanging up.

Hmmm, I could fly down there. How hard would it be to randomly run into him, strike up a conversation, and then hope to spend time with him to get to know his character? She thought for a few minutes, watching the wind race through her rose garden, dropping petals to the ground.

Flowers . . . Aha! That's it! His wife! Maybe there's an in through his wife!

Ariel called Greg's house phone.

"Hi. I'm not home. Leave a message." It was a man's voice on the recorder.

A few more minutes of empty thought slipped by when her phone rang.

"Stuart, I don't think he's married . . ." Ariel answered Stuart's call, starting right in, running through ideas. "And he's at the hospital working over lunch. If he had been married, I'd talk with his wife first, like deliver flowers or something and strike up a conversation."

Stuart interrupted, "Dating sites." The words rolled right off his tongue. "A single workaholic, lives in a small town, not much goin' on. He'll want a release."

"Stuart, have you ever thought there could be one man on the planet who doesn't just think with his—"

"He's called dead," Stuart interrupted.

"Fun-ny, Stuart," Ariel chided.

"Let me rephrase . . . I did it. I went on dating sites sometimes."

"Wouldn't you imagine his best foot would be forward on one of those things? It's pretty much the same as an interview." She leaned on the windowsill watching the river slip along. Then she opened her laptop.

"True," he said. "Ariel, I can hear you typing. What are you doing over there?"

"What'd ya think? Obviously, looking at dating sites."

Stuart laughed. "Make a profile, my sweet nothing," he practically sang.

"Give me a break. I'm not really gonna look for him there."

"Give it a go, might get lucky," Stuart teased a bit more.

"You do it! Maybe he's interested in rugged, smarty-pants men," she retorted.

"No problem," Stuart said. "I'm open to adventure. Here's a site."

"Is he on there?" Ariel asked.

"Don't know... setting up an account now," Stuart told her.

"How?" she asked.

"Pay twenty-five bucks and post a picture. I think I have some." His keyboard clicked away through the phone receiver.

"I wonder how many people are on these things just to people watch?" Ariel wondered aloud.

"What should I call myself?" Stuart asked.

"Seeking Dr. G.?" Ariel laughed lightheartedly.

"Miss Chocolat." Stuart's laughter teased back.

"No!" Ariel's voice was firm. "I thought you were making your own profile. You're strikingly handsome. What man wouldn't think twice?"

"Well, there are definitely men that would think twice, but I'm engaged, so it's your turn at the plate. You're up!"

"No pictures!" Ariel sugarcoated her demand. "Have mercy on him."

"Come on, Ariel. You're a beautiful, mysterious lady. Dark hair and hazel—I mean dirt—eyes. They are a little small, but you've got an infectious smile. Think of this as another adventure for the soul." He laughed again. "Login stuff is in your inbox—

let's go fishing."

A few minutes of entertainment scrolling through pictures with Stuart left her choking.

"This is . . ."Ariel coughed on a laugh. "I think . . . Wait, I think I found him. Stuart, I think it's him!"

"Are you kidding me?" A hint of pride registered in his voice. "Knew he would be on here . . ."

"Just don't click his profile. I think he'll see we looked at him," Ariel guessed as she said it.

"Too late, too late. You looked at him."

"Dang it, Stuart." She sighed.

"Who knows—"

"You're not quite being helpful."

"Oh, Ariel, lighten up. Laugh a little! One day these sites will be full of people that want to meet a friend. One day, this is how most people will meet."

"We're going to Orlando in a few weeks. Just drive over to meet him if you haven't been able to talk to him by then," Stuart suggested.

"Okay, can you delete this account for me?" Ariel asked.

"Sure thing. Good night, Madam Chocolate. Tell those

young men hello for me when they get home."

"I'll tell 'em. Good night," Ariel said quietly. "I'm glad you met someone to share your life with. You really are a special person."

Now that was a terrible . . . strange dream. A fading image of Stuart hosting the Dating Game slipped away with the rising sun. Steam rushed from a large mug of steeping grapefruit tea. Her inbox chimed awake with emails.

Oh great, it wasn't a dream. Stuart, you didn't delete it! While the messages moved from inbox to trash with a single click of the mouse, a message came in. A message from Greg.

"Okay, what do I say to this?" Her leg bounced repetitively as it often did when she was thinking.

Dear Greg,

Thank you for your note. To answer your question, my life does seem to have chocolate or cocoa lacing throughout it. And, as you noted, yes, I do live about as far away from Sarasota as possible in the continental US, over 3000 miles. I'd never been on a site like this before and my friend and I were curious to see how they worked. He was the one who made my profile - kind of as a joke, I thought he'd deleted it for me (within the hour of making it). If you ever want to talk though, you are welcome to call. — Ariel

And with that email sent, she deleted the account.

A Simple Twist of Chocolate

In the afternoon when her phone rang, Greg spoke for almost an hour while Ariel listened. It was a typical first-time conversation, defaulting into a brief version of his resume.

"I have a PhD in Molecular Biology and decided on becoming a medical oncologist and hematologist. Looked at several jobs before deciding on Sarasota. I went to George Washington University, went to medical school in Israel, studied at Johns Hopkins, did my residency in San Diego, and here I am ten years later." He made some forays into a backstory here and there, adding a little color. "I'm online because I like conversation. I talk to many women all over. I've been talking with some of them for years now and never met them in person. Nothing sexual, just conversations. I've even had business partners I've never met in person. Just over the phone."

"That's interesting." Ariel couldn't quite think of anything else to say at that point, so she just kept listening.

Then Greg said, "I say this to all the women I do meet, though. I tell them all the same thing: Don't go picking out curtains or anything, because I'm not interested in a relationship like that."

"Well, you don't have to worry about me picking out curtains for us. I'm just interested in conversation also; I like to learn," Ariel said, breaking in. "And today, I've learned quite a bit. So, for now, I need to go."

"Can we talk again tomorrow?" he asked.

"I suppose. Don't you need to work, though?"

"It's 7 p.m. here. It's you who should be working," he said.

"Touché. I'd better get working then."

***

Ariel paced the length of her living room, her phone pressed to her ear. Greg's voice was clear on the other end, calm and measured as always. He had that way of speaking that made it seem like he was letting you in on some great secret, even when he wasn't saying much at all.

"I have to admit," Ariel said, letting a note of curiosity seep into her tone, "your background is fascinating. Oncology, biotech investments—it's not exactly a common combination."

Greg chuckled softly. "I've always believed medicine and technology should go hand in hand. If we're not pushing for innovation, we're just reacting. I prefer to be ahead of the game."

"And you're clearly succeeding," Ariel replied, keeping her voice light. "But what made you pick oncology in the first place? It's not an easy field."

Greg was quiet for a second, and Ariel imagined him in his car heading to the tennis courts, considering how much to share. "I like a challenge," he said finally. "And oncology is nothing if not challenging. But also, I chose medicine because as much as I love working in the lab, there was no money in it. There isn't much money in medicine either unless you own the practice or are a partner." Not wanting to make his career choice sound entirely money-driven, he added, "You know, there's meaning in it, in oncology, real stakes. You're not just treating symptoms; you're fighting for lives."

Ariel nodded to herself, letting the sincerity in his tone settle before pressing on. "And yet you've taken that expertise beyond medicine," she said, steering the conversation carefully. "Biotech investments aren't exactly a natural extension for most oncologists. What drew you in?"

Greg's laugh was lighter this time, more casual. "Let's just say I saw an opportunity. Technology is where the breakthroughs happen—new treatments, diagnostics, even predictive analytics. It's all about making medicine smarter, and being able to buy it in bulk."

"And I'm guessing that's how you got involved with Clymenos?" Ariel asked, the question delivered so casually it almost sounded offhand.

Greg didn't respond immediately, and she heard the faint rustle of paper on his end. "You've done your homework," he said finally, a hint of amusement in his voice.

"Well, they're hard to miss," Ariel replied. "Big name, big reputation—especially in biotech circles. What's your connection to them?"

"It started with a friend," Greg said, his voice shifting to something more thoughtful. "He's a brilliant guy, developed a medical analytics platform that could change how we predict treatment outcomes. But getting it off the ground was a nightmare. Investors were interested, but not enough to take it past the prototype stage."

"So, you brought it to Clymenos," Ariel said, filling in the blanks.

"Exactly," Greg confirmed. "They have the resources and the network to make things happen. It's a win-win: my friend gets the support he needs, and I get to be part of something that could transform oncology as we know it."

Ariel let his words hang for a moment before speaking again. "And how's it going? Working with a group like Clymenos can't be easy."

"They're... particular," Greg admitted. "I respect that. They know what they want, and they don't waste time getting it. Honestly, it's refreshing. Too many people in this field hesitate when it's time to make hard decisions. And to tell you the truth, I don't actually work for them. I wish I did. I just brought my friend to their attention. Ultimately nothing happened between me and them, though. My friend is not easy to work with, and Clymenos doesn't like headaches."

"True," Ariel said, her voice thoughtful. "But that kind of

focus sometimes comes with strings attached. Have you ever run into any?"

Greg's tone cooled just slightly. "Everything comes with strings, Ariel. You just have to know how to pull them before they pull you."

"Let's just say I'm comfortable creating my own complexity," Greg said smoothly. "And honestly, I think that's why we get along so well. You're sharp. You get it."

The rhythmic thwack of tennis balls echoed in the background, Ariel leaned back on the nearby bench, phone pressed to her ear, half-listening to Greg's voice as he got ready to play.

"You wouldn't believe it, Ariel," he said, pausing to wipe sweat from his brow. "Gabe took me to Italy—Tuscany, actually. He wanted me to see the wineries, the way the land was cultivated, how the estates were managed. He said it was inspiration for the resort in the DR, a model he wanted to replicate. He really gets it, you know? He sees potential where others don't."

"Who is Gabe?" She asked, confused with this jump in topic and not having the name associated with Clymenos.

"My business partner in the Dominican Republic." He responded as though it was well known.

Ariel made a noncommittal noise, pen in hand, absently

scribbling loops onto the margins of an old receipt.

"And the way he does business—it's refreshing," Greg continued. "No bureaucratic nonsense, no layers of paperwork, just trust. He says real businessmen don't need contracts—only cowards do. Everything's done on a handshake."

Her hand paused mid-loop.

"I mean, look, you know how people get caught up in legalese and end up missing out on real opportunities? Gabe's different. He believes in loyalty, in partnership." His voice dipped lower, almost conspiratorial. "He calls me his brother, Ariel. That means something."

His stories settled into Ariel's mind like stones on water, sending out ripples that overlapped with past conversations, past inconsistencies.

She remained silent, listening as he rattled on about vineyard estates, yacht meetings, and whispered assurances of returns that defied logic.

And then he said it.

"I mean, yeah, I send him money, but it's an investment," Greg reasoned. "He shows me the Dominican accounts—money moving, deals happening. It's all transparent."

As she hung up, Ariel let out a slow breath. The pieces of the puzzle were falling into place. Greg was sharper than most in some ways, but in others, he could be swayed easier than most too. She'd have to tread carefully if she wanted to uncover the full extent of his involvement with Clymenos—and Red Genesis.

"You know," Ariel said when Stuart called, "I did find out some stuff about him while I was researching his background. He is trying to fund a company of his own called ENSA, Environmentally Sustainable Agriculture. It's a rice project in the Dominican Republic. He is also on this other website for a service called Sacred Rights of the Ganges, helping Hindus return family members' ashes to the Ganges River in Varanasi from the United States. I mean, the list goes on. Another project is for a sustainable sturgeon fish farm for caviar." She paused, then said, "I wonder if he needs investors for the ENSA project. I know a few people looking to invest in something along those lines. And it's a great excuse for an in-person meeting."

Chapter Seventeen

Cocoa must be handled with gentle prudence. It increases cognitive unity, and it opens the pathways toward a profound connection with eternal life.

My mind started wandering in faraway thoughts and my words to our little group followed close behind. "Did you know Dr. Hans-Peter Dürr, former head of the Max Planck Institute for Physics in Munich, says, 'What we consider the here and now, this world, is actually just the material level that is comprehensible.' I personally believe the beyond is an infinite reality that is much bigger. I often refer to it as a magnificent symphony, and this life experience we are undergoing now is but a mere note within it. Our lives in this realm of existence are encompassed, surrounded by the ethereal world already. The body dies, but the spiritual quantum field continues. In this way, we are immortal."

Shaking myself back into the present, I said, "Let's continue with Greg…"

* * *

Ariel's phone buzzed against the kitchen counter, cutting through the late-afternoon quiet. Ariel glanced at the screen: "Greg Denslock." She picked it up, cradling it between shoulder and ear as she stirred a pot of simmering tea. For a month now, he had been calling her daily after work.

"Hey, Greg," she said, her voice warm but edged with purpose. "Good timing—I've got news. I know a few people who might invest in ENSA. They're up here, free next week to hear a pitch. What's your schedule like?"

"That's great, Ariel. I can't make it out there myself—too much on my plate—but I'll send my CFO, CAO, and CEO. They can handle the presentation. Will that work?"

She rolled her eyes — *it's you I need to see.* "Of course. I'm sure they'll be fine."

"Thanks."

She set the spoon down, leaning against the counter, the faint scent of chamomile rising around her. "Speaking of help, I've got a few questions—about your Caribbean projects. The resort, the winery, that 'yellow pages' building you mentioned."

"Yeah?" Greg's tone shifted, curiosity threading through it.

"What about them?"

"You got a minute?" She slid into a chair, voice settling into a rhythm that said, Stay with me. "You know I used to consult—still do, sometimes—for a private outfit. We dug into everything: embezzlement, tax schemes, international fraud; corporate missteps hiding in plain sight—insider trades, misused funds, you name it." Her fingers traced the rim of her mug; her tone was casual despite the weight. "Not all doom and gloom, though—there were lighter gigs too."

"Lighter?"

"Yeah," she said, a laugh bubbling up. "There was a time I hunted cocoa in the rainforest. That was a good one."

"Cocoa?" His chair creaked faintly in the background.

"Not just any cocoa," she said, her smile audible. "A client swore there was a lost strain out there—pure, rich, practically mythical. Antioxidants off the charts, a subtle taste you couldn't fake. He even claimed it tied back to ancient rituals, like something out of a storybook. Stuart and I chased it for months—mud up to our knees, bugs everywhere, chasing whispers through Panama and Venezuela."

Greg chuckled, "You're telling me you trekked through jungles for chocolate?"

"Something like that," she said, her voice softening with

memory. "It wasn't all glamour—mostly dead ends and sweaty nights."

"Did you find it?" His question came quick, almost eager.

"Well. We found something. A rare strain, maybe not the legend, but close enough to make you wonder. The real treasure was the hunt itself—the people, the puzzle, the way it all fit together."

Greg exhaled, a sound that carried a mix of amusement and respect. "So, there's a stash of mythical chocolate hidden somewhere?"

"Not quite," she teased. "It was an old man's fairy tale, but it taught me to look deeper. Which brings me back to the Caribbean—I'd like to hear more about what you are working on."

His tone shifted, a touch guarded. "What are you getting at? You don't trust the projects?"

"I'm just curious. After all, you call Gabe Acero 'your brother.' How'd you meet him?"

"He's my oncology partner's nephew," Greg replied, a hint of pride seeping in. "Good guy—sees the value I bring."

Ariel nodded to herself, filing that away. "I'll bet his other ventures are interesting too. Is it hard to read the reports and financials, or does he give you copies in English?"

"I translate them the best I can. I don't speak Spanish but know enough key words to make sense of things. And my oncology partner is from Columbia and her husband is Dominican, so I rely on them quite a bit to translate."

A pause crackled through the line, then Greg's voice hardened. "Gabe's solid. I've worked my ass off to build what I have, and he gets that. He's not some con artist—he's loyal, straightforward. We've traveled together, Ariel. That's not manipulation; that's respect."

She stayed quiet, letting him roll on, sensing the edge beneath his words.

"I'm not saying you're wrong to ask," he added, softening slightly. "I trust you with this stuff—that's why I let you peek at it. But Gabe's not the problem here. He's not out to screw me over. You might see red flags, but I see a partner. Can we leave it at that?"

"Okay," she said, her tone easing, though her mind didn't. "I'm in Orlando this week. Early dinner sound good?"

Greg brightened, a grin creeping into his voice. "How about the weekend? I've got a guest room—no hotel needed. Nothing weird, just a friend crashing. My sister stays over all the time."

She hesitated, weighing it. "Let's stick with dinner for now, okay? We'll see how it goes."

"No pressure," he said, smooth and easy. "Offer's open—parents, best friend, they all crash here. Same deal."

"Got it," she said. "Dinner it is."

Ariel set the phone down, her tea gone cold.

***

The rental car's engine purred beneath Stuart's hands as he eased onto I-4, the Orlando skyline shrinking into a haze of glass and steel in the rearview mirror. Ariel sat beside him, her head resting against the passenger window, the late afternoon sun catching the edges of her dark hair. Palm trees streaked past in a green blur, their fronds swaying against the sky.

"So," he said, his voice light but pointed, "Greg."

Ariel shifted, her arms crossing as she turned her head just enough to meet his gaze. "What about him?"

Stuart grinned, a quick flash that didn't quite hide his curiosity. "Come on, Ariel. You've been chewing on something since that call. I can practically hear the gears turning. What's your take?"

She sighed, settling back into the seat, her fingers tapping a slow rhythm against her elbow. "He's smart. More than just a doctor, it is his brilliance is in biotech that stands out. But, he lacks wisdom, and likes to tell stories." Her brow creased, voice dipping. "He doesn't fit the Clymenos mold." Her gaze drifted back to the window, the passing trees a fleeting canvas for her thoughts. "They're precision—cold, calculated, every step scripted. Greg's a storyteller—sweeping visions, big ideas, gossip. It's magnetic, sure, but Clymenos doesn't want charmers. They want operators—quiet, controlled, no flair."

Stuart nodded, his fingers tightening slightly on the wheel. "You think they checked him out, though?"

"Guaranteed," she said, her voice firm, almost cutting. "Someone like him doesn't ping their radar without a deep dive. But I'd wager they passed. He's too independent—wouldn't take orders, wouldn't play by their rules. If they'd offered him a spot, he'd have demanded the reins, and Clymenos doesn't bend for that."

"Interesting," Stuart mused, his eyes flicking to the road then back to her. "Yet he's tangled up with them through that analytics project."

"Was," Ariel corrected, leaning forward, her voice gaining an edge. "They pulled back—declined to invest in his friend's company. I'm starting to think that 'investment interest' was just a smoke screen, a way to vet him without tipping their hand."

Stuart's brow lifted, a spark of amusement in his glance. "Maybe he's playing them too. Doesn't trust them any more than they trust him."

A faint smirk curled her lips, sharp and knowing. "That'd fit. He's not one to give up control—thrives on being the wildcard. It's his edge, and he knows it."

The car drove quietly, the skyline now a memory behind them, replaced by sprawling suburbs and the faint shimmer of heat rising off the road. Stuart shot her another look, his tone shifting to a tease. "So, what's the move? You just gonna keep dissecting him in that head of yours, or you got a plan?"

Ariel didn't answer right away, her gaze locked on the horizon where the sun sank low. When she spoke, her voice was calm, resolute, a river carving its path. "I'm driving to Sarasota tomorrow. Meeting him face-to-face."

Stuart's hands twitched on the wheel, his head snapping toward her. "You're what?"

"You heard me." She turned, meeting his stare, her eyes steady despite the flicker of doubt beneath them. "I've circled this too long. I need to read him up close—face-to-face. If I wait for the perfect moment, it'll never come."

Stuart's mouth quirked, caught between a frown and a grin. "You know this is a bad idea, right?"

"I know," she said. "I won't push. But, I have to go. No loose ends, Stuart—we can't afford them. And there's more. Those Caribbean projects—he's being scammed. Millions. Gabe

Acero's got him sending every bonus, every paycheck after expenses, blind as a bat. Money laundering, drug trade stuff."

Stuart's brow lifted as he parked, turning to her fully. "How'd you dig that up?"

"Remember Peralta?" she said, stepping out as he followed. "Dominican Republic, bulk cash runs a few years back? Same network. Julio poked around Santo Domingo—Gabe's tied to a port building, arms-length from the cash, but it's dirty. With the projects Greg is involved in, at least $25 millions flowed through his accounts... mostly Greg's and his oncology partner's. Wired to Gabe's Wells Fargo in Miami, then Panama. Greg thinks it's land deals—Gabe's billing him millions for parcels worth thousands."

Stuart held the restaurant door, whistling low. "A handshake scam?"

"Exactly." She slipped inside, her voice quickening as they neared the table. "Gabe buys the land cheap, titles it, then fakes a sale to Greg for millions. That port building? Shoddy as a movie set—Greg's cash could've built a skyscraper. Every time Gabe asks, Greg sends more—life savings, Stuart."

He slid into the booth, eyes narrowing. "And the port's Gabe's real play?"

"Under aliases, yeah," she said, settling across from him. "He's dangling resorts, ninety-times returns—feeding Greg's greed, or some need I can't pin down. Land prices he's charging could buy Manhattan penthouses, and Greg just keeps writing checks."

Stuart leaned back, shaking his head. "You're walking into a lion's den to save a guy who won't thank you."

"Maybe," she said, her gaze drifting to the window, the horizon now a bruise of dusk. "But if I don't, who will?"

***

Like clockwork, Greg called later than night, "I dreamt of you yesterday."

"Oh? Was it bad?" Ariel asked.

"You laced some cocoa with a mind-controlling substance. And you're actually coming here to harvest my kidneys," Greg told her, loving a good conspiracy. "Well, you weren't doing the surgery. You were just in charge."

"Darn," she dramatized, "you uncovered our diabolical plan! The team and I were coming out to coerce you to eat more chocolate. Then, once you're in a doped-up cocoa trance, whack! But we were only going to take one of 'em this time. That's why I'm coming in a few days early."

"You are? Great. When?"

"Tomorrow."

"Tomorrow! I'll leave the door open. I'll be there around seven, after work."

The rhythmic thwack of tennis balls echoed across the court, accompanied by the occasional grunt of exertion and the scuffle of sneakers against the outdoor court surface. Greg stood at the baseline, bouncing the ball once, twice, before launching it into a smooth serve.

"Nice shot," his tennis partner, Sam, called out as he lunged to return it, the ball zipping just over the net.

Greg moved quickly, sending the ball sailing back with a precise backhand. "Thanks," he replied, smirking. "You'll miss the next one, though."

Sam rolled his eyes and charged toward the ball. He managed a decent return, but Greg was already anticipating it, smashing a volley down the line for the point.

"Unbelievable," Sam muttered, wiping his forehead with the back of his hand. "How can you even see through all that sweat?"

Greg chuckled, bouncing the ball lazily on the court. "It's all about control. Anticipation. It's not that hard when you—"

"Yeah, yeah, spare me the lecture," Sam cut in, retrieving the ball. "So, what's this I hear about you leaving your front door open for some woman you've never met?"

Greg raised an eyebrow, tossing the ball in the air. "What's the big deal? She's stopping by this afternoon, and I won't be home. Figured it'd be easier for her to let herself in. She might stay the night too."

Sam stared at him like he'd grown an extra head. "You're insane. Do you just invite strangers into your house like it's some kind of open house?"

"She's not a stranger," Greg said defensively, sending another serve rocketing over the net.

"You've only talked to her on the phone," Sam shot back, missing the return entirely. He pointed his racket at Greg like it was a sword. "That counts as stranger territory."

Greg smirked. "We've spoken almost daily. Besides, I have nothing to hide."

Sam let out a laugh that was more of a bark. "Right. Until you come home and your silverware's missing. Or worse, she finds something incriminating, and you end up on the evening news."

Greg rolled his eyes. "Please. Ariel's not like that."

Sam shook his head, leaning on his racket. "You're lucky I like you, because this? This is a bad idea. I hope you've at least thought to lock up the good stuff."

Greg waved him off. "You worry too much. It'll be fine."

"Sure, until it isn't," Sam muttered as they switched sides of the court. "I can't wait to say I told you so."

After tennis, Greg returned home, a thin layer of sweat clinging to his skin. Greg pulled into his driveway, his tennis bag slung over one shoulder, sweat clinging to him like a second skin. Stepping through the side gate, he paused for a moment, looking toward the pool, the water shimmering under the bright morning light.

He dropped his bag on a patio chair and tugged off his shirt, the fabric sticking briefly before he flung it over the back of the chair. His shoes and socks followed, then his shorts, until he stood there in nothing but the breeze brushing against his skin.

Greg glanced toward the fence that separated his yard from the neighbors', an easy smirk playing on his lips. "If they're watching, they're welcome," he muttered to himself. "Not my fault they can't mind their own business."

With that, he walked to the edge of the pool, the concrete warm under his feet, and jumped in. The cool water enveloped him instantly, washing away the heat of the morning and the sweat from the game. He surfaced in the middle of the pool, running his hands over the smooth shave of his bald head as he floated for a moment, his eyes closed against the sun.

For a man who spent so much of his time in calculated control, Greg relished moments like this—simple, unplanned, indulgent. He walked a few lazy laps, enjoying the weightlessness of the water, before finally hoisting himself onto the edge of the pool.

With a shake of his head, Greg stood and walked back toward the house, unapologetically bare to the world. He grabbed a towel from the patio, slinging it around his waist before heading inside. The house was quiet, save for the faint hum of the air conditioning, and Greg relished the solitude as he made his way to the bathroom. He stepped into the shower, the cool water cascading over him as he ran through his mental checklist for the day. Work, meetings, emails—and Ariel.

Twenty minutes later, freshly dressed in a crisp shirt and tie, Greg moved through the house with purpose. He paused in his home office, scanning the room. For someone with nothing to hide, there were still things he'd rather not leave lying around.

His personal files—financial statements, contracts, correspondence—were stacked neatly in a corner. He grabbed the pile, tucking it under his arm as he reached for his checkbooks and the small lockbox where he kept emergency cash.

"This is ridiculous," he muttered to himself, but he didn't stop.

Carrying everything out to the garage, Greg opened the trunk of his car and placed the items inside. After a moment's thought, he grabbed a beach towel from the back seat and threw it over the stack. It didn't look particularly secure, but it was better than nothing.

He straightened, dusting his hands off as though the act of stashing his belongings had been physically demanding. "There," he said aloud. "Safe and sound."

As he climbed into the driver's seat, he couldn't help but think of Sam's teasing voice. *You're lucky I like you, because this is a bad idea.*

Greg gave a quick chortle, smiling faintly as he backed out of the driveway. "It's not a bad idea," he told himself. "It's just . . . precautionary."

The white of his front door blurred behind a fine sheen of pollen and humidity. A cool rush of air greeted her as she pushed it open, carrying with it the soft perfume of orchids, their petals luminous in the high-ceilinged, sunlit room. Inside, tapestries hung like whispers. Antique desks and tables stood solemnly in their places, watching her, curious. The room was filled with conspirators in quiet conversation.

Ariel stepped lightly, careful not to disturb them. She moved toward the wrought iron banister with purpose, but she couldn't help feeling the way the room shifted around her, its attention settling momentarily on the intruder. Everything had eyes, watching, waiting, observing her as she ascended the stairs.

A Simple Twist of Chocolate

When she reached the guest room, she placed her bag on the dresser and surveyed the space. The bed stood neatly made, its crisp linens folded with the kind of precision that suggested the hands of someone who cared deeply about such details. Ariel sat on the edge, the mattress yielding slightly beneath her weight, and reached for her book of crosswords.

Somewhere between five across and nine down, the room's murmurings faded, and the world softened at the edges. The book slipped from her hand, falling against the bedspread, its pages half-open as though still waiting for her to return. She drifted off, her breathing steady, the stillness of the house enveloping her like a warm quilt.

A voice startled her awake, cutting sharply through the quiet like a crack of thunder on a calm day. It called from the front door, rising up the staircase and into the room, pulling her from her half-formed dreams. Ariel sat up quickly, her heart racing, her mind scrambling to get her bearings.

"Honey, I'm home!" It sounded like George from the Honeymooners.

Jumping from the bed and flying through the small sitting area, she came to a screeching halt atop the stairwell. Greg stood at the bottom, eyes shining like polished tiger's eye crystals against tanned skin. At a stocky five feet, nine inches, his bald head gave him a more commanding presence. His hand guided her down like she was Vanna White. "You look just as I imagined. Did you find your way here without getting lost?" he asked.

They awkwardly hugged.

"I made reservations for dinner. You hungry?" he asked. Ariel nodded.

The patio air softened as the thick humidity eased, a waiter guiding them to a table strung with fairy lights. Ariel's fingers brushed her water glass, knocking it. Ice clattered, water pooling across the tablecloth.

"Careful!" Greg jumped back.

"Oh! I'm so sorry!" she gasped, hands fumbling to right it, her face flushing. "I didn't mean—"

"Didn't think it was on purpose," he teased, leaning back, watching her scramble. "Nervous?"

"No, I'm fine."

While trying to convince herself that she was fine, she unrolled her napkin, sending the flatware skyward, before they corrected their course and crashed upon the table. *What is wrong with me?* "This looks like a nice place to eat," she said, pretending nothing out of the ordinary had happened.

Disbelief doused his expression. "I've been here a few times, It's fairly good." He leaned in a little, "Ariel, what is it that you do, exactly?"

"Well...." She wriggled in her seat. Her fingers twisted her necklace, words slipping away—what is wrong with me? Come on, Ariel, Straighten up.

"Got any floss?" he cut in, his grin playful, eyes sharp.

"What?" She looked at him haloed in light from the streetlamp, she needed to snap out of it.

"Floss." he repeated, slower, "Have any?"

She patted her dress—no pockets, no escape—her napkin now a tight knot in her lap. "No, sorry... I don't."

By the time the never-ending dinner was over, Greg got up from the table, making it a point to step aside just in case she had sent it toppling. "Ready to go?"

"Sure," she replied in relief.

"Why did you want to get into chocolate instead of consulting?" he asked her as they pulled into his driveway. "But you're still consulting a bit now, though, right?"

"Yes, I am still consulting. As for the cacao, I guess because it makes people feel good," she answered, waiting for him to unlock the front door.

"My guard frog." Greg pointed to a large frog, moon-bathing on the windowsill. "What are you working on now?"

"He's cute. Does he bite?" she asked, touching the frog's back.

"No."

"I'm not working on anything too exciting," she said. "Just interviewing people for a client. I don't mean to cut our evening short, but would it be okay if we call it a night? I'm pretty wiped out."

"No problem," he said, leaning in for a kiss.

She extended her hand instead. "Until tomorrow, then. Good night."

Over the course of the next few months Ariel made several more trips to Sarasota and gently approached the subject of Gabe and the Dominican Republic investment. Each attempt was slammed shut with a one-sided heated argument. Greg would say, "You have no idea what you are talking about. I researched the investment before I sent money down. Plus, Gabe considers me family; he calls me his brother." Or "I think it's best if you go home if you want to keep telling me these lies. You have no idea what you are talking about."

Ariel finally dropped the subject until the day Greg took her to the airport. As they were on the way, he said, "I want you to go meet Gabe. I'll get you a ticket to the DR and a hotel room. He will pick you up at the airport. You'll see he is a good guy."

And so, a month later, when Brandon was visiting Gresham over a school break, Ariel went. It was an interesting trip. Gabe showed Ariel the commercial buildings in Santo Domingo, he showed her the port location he was planning on purchasing, and then he took her to the south coast where the vineyard and future resort property were located. Ariel listened as Gabe and his wife pitched the project. They didn't request money from Ariel outright, but they were clearly trying to entice her to ask if she could invest. She did not. Instead, she got him talking about Greg. At one point, Gabe told her Greg was very, very wealthy and had plenty of money to lose.

"I don't believe Greg has as much money as you think he has." Ariel leaned in slightly, lowering her voice and making him listen closely.

"Oh, he has much money. He is a famous doctor," Gabe replied.

"He does not have the amount of money you are hoping he has. He is sending you everything he makes. All of his bonuses, everything."

"He wouldn't be that dumb," Gabe said flatly. "No one would do that."

"You need to stop asking him for money," Ariel said just as flatly.

"He wants to give me his money. Who am I to say no? He asked me to invest the money. He came to me."

On the final day, Gabe and his wife took Ariel to dinner before her flight.

"Who are you?" he asked Ariel.

"A friend of Greg's."

"I don't think so. I had an associate look into you, and we can't find anything. Who do you work for? Are you with the American government?"

Ariel didn't answer.

"Do you have a gun? Have you ever killed anyone?" Gabe asked seriously.

"I have never killed anyone." Ariel cocked her head slightly. "Is there a reason you are worried about this?"

Gabe looked at his wife and then back to Ariel. "I am just not someone you want to play with, that is all. You don't want to play with us."

Ariel took a slow sip of her drink, letting Gabe's last words hang in the air between them. The restaurant was dimly lit, the murmur of conversation from other tables filling the space like background static. She set her glass down with deliberate ease, meeting Gabe's gaze without a flicker of hesitation.

"Play with you?" she echoed, a small, amused smile tugging at the corner of her lips. "Gabe, if I were playing, you'd already know the rules."

His wife shifted uncomfortably beside him, but Gabe held Ariel's stare, studying her. Testing.

"You think I don't know what I'm doing?" he asked, his voice low.

"Oh, I'm sure you do," Ariel said smoothly. She leaned in just enough to make him feel the shift. "That's what makes this so fascinating." She tapped a nail against the rim of her glass. "But let me offer you a bit of free advice—if you're smart, you'll take it. Stop while you're ahead."

Gabe's jaw twitched. "And if I don't?"

Ariel tilted her head considering his question. An undercurrent rippled from within tiding deep resolve which touched the corners of her mouth. "Then I suppose we'll both find out exactly who we're dealing with."

Gabe didn't respond right away. He glanced at his wife, who gave him a subtle, almost imperceptible shake of her head. Whatever he saw in Ariel's expression—or whatever he couldn't see—was enough to make him shift back in his seat.

After a moment, he let out a short breath and picked up his fork. "Enjoy your dinner, Ariel."

She took another sip of her drink, her smile unwavering. "I plan to."

***

Later that night, in their penthouse suite overlooking the city, Gabe poured himself a glass of dark rum, swirling it absently as he stared out at the skyline. His wife sat cross-legged on the sleek leather couch, scrolling through something with a concentrated frown.

"She's a problem," Gabe's wife said.

Gabe exhaled sharply, taking a slow sip before setting his glass down with more force than necessary. "No kidding." He turned to face her. "She's not just some nosy friend. And the way she looked at me tonight? She wasn't scared. She was studying me."

His wife grunted in agreement, still scrolling. "She doesn't have an online footprint, no family connections we can trace. That's not normal. Either she's someone important, or someone's protecting her." She glanced up, meeting Gabe's gaze. "You think she's with the government?"

Gabe scoffed. "Maybe. But she denied it too easily. Like she wanted me to believe she was something worse." He ran a hand over his jaw, mind turning. "Either way, she's got Greg's ear, and that's a problem. He was already hesitant about sending more money. If she keeps pushing, he might actually grow a spine."

His wide leaned back, crossing her arms. "Then we need to make sure he stops talking to her."

Gabe smirked. "And how do you propose we do that?"

She set her phone down, eyes gleaming with something sharp. "We make her the villain."

He arched an eyebrow. "Go on."

"She's already an enigma. We use that. Make Greg doubt her. Feed him little pieces of information—imply she has her own agenda, that she's lying to him." She uncrossed her legs and leaned forward. "We don't tell him outright. We let him discover it. A well-placed warning from you, an 'old friend.' A casual mention that we ran a background check and found... nothing." She tilted her head. "No real past? That alone will make him wonder who she really is. You know how his imagination gets the better of him."

Gabe rubbed his chin, considering. "And if he doesn't take the bait?"

She smiled. "Then we make her a threat."

Gabe's smirk widened. "You're beautiful when you're devious, you know that?"

She picked up her phone again, her voice light, almost

amused as she looked at the screen. "I do."

Chapter Eighteen

The fraying of twine begins simply, one tiny break at a time. Maybe the process ambles, maybe it happens quickly, but one thing is for certain: once it starts, it's nearly impossible to stop.

"Greg, how well do you know Gabe?" Ariel asked, floating around in the pool at Greg's house while Brandon played lacrosse for the afternoon with one of the local clubs they had found for kids his age.

"Why do you keep asking me this? I consider him my brother," Greg said, leaning on the pool's edge.

"Do you know he thinks you are very wealthy, like you have millions of dollars to lose? That you are only giving him a fraction of what you make," Ariel said gently, as casually as she could.

"You don't know what you are talking about. He knows I am just a doctor. I sent you there so you could see he is a good guy."

"Yes, he does know that you are a doctor. 'A famous doctor,' he says... I need you to tell you something, okay? He isn't the man you think he is. He launders money for the cartel, and all the money you send to him is headed to Panama. Next time he asks for money, say no. Just see what happens."

Greg tensed. "You don't know what you are talking about. Who do you think you are?"

Ariel stopped her leisurely float and stood in the shallow water. "You know, I am telling you this because I don't like to see people taken advantage of. And I consider you my friend. I am standing up for you because I do not want to see you hurt more than you've already been. The resort project is a way to embezzle and launder money. Gabe is not a good guy."

"He's my brother."

"Okay," Ariel said, "That's what he says, but he doesn't really care. When you go down there, and you stay at his house, I bet he is billing you for that, for the food, for the pickup from the airport, the helicopter rides, all of it. And then what about the tunnel?" Gabe had told Ariel that he was building a tunnel connecting two parking lots, one of which had yet to be built. The tunnel had been blasted about one-tenth of the distance and then never resumed or completed, yet he still charged Greg for the construction. "It is not real; he is taking advantage of you. He is stealing your money."

"You don't know what you are talking about," Greg said so firmly that Ariel dropped the subject.

For almost a year, Ariel and Stuart worked on their project, handing it off when their jobs were complete. They also kept an eye on Gabe out of curiosity and started to put together a picture of who that criminal was. For the most part, Ariel tried relaying the information as gently as she could to Greg, but he remained steadfast. He adamantly stood his ground and continued sending hundreds of thousands of dollars to Gabe each time he asked.

Over the course of the year, Ariel found herself making a point to visit Greg whenever her travels sent her in his direction. With Brandon by her side—soaking in the world as she unschooled him—their little detours became an unspoken tradition. Each visit with Greg felt like stepping into a different rhythm, a pause from the intensity of her work and the fluidity of her nomadic life.

She had tried more than once to explain how they met, to tell him the real reason she had sought him out in the first place. But every time she broached the topic, Greg brushed it aside with a dismissive laugh or a quick change of subject. "Come on, Ariel," he'd say, smirking. "You can't expect me to believe that."

At first, she'd pressed him, trying to find the right words to make him understand. But over time, she let it go. Maybe it was easier for him to believe it was all coincidence, some amusing twist of fate that had brought her into his life. And maybe he needed that—just like he needed Gabe to remain the larger-than-life figure his imagination had conjured.

Greg's life was complicated enough, and Ariel had no desire to add to his burdens. Instead, accepting their friendship it for what it was: imperfect, layered, and strangely comforting in its unpredictability.

Brandon found Greg amusing. The tales about his career, his travels, or some obscure piece of knowledge that only Greg could make sound like the most important thing in the world.

Then one day, in a small French café in Sarasota, Florida, while Ariel was visiting, the threads began to unravel. Greg was in the middle of telling one of his childhood tales.

"Tom and I must've been about eleven when we were at temple on the day of repentance, Yom Kippur. Bored and hungry, we slipped into the coat closet to check people's pockets for candy or anything to eat. Old mothballs and peppermint—that's what the air in there tasted like. And the only light was through the crack of the door." Greg started smiling guiltily as he was telling the story. "'I bet they don't even know we're in here. What'd ya think, Greg?' Tom asked me, crawling under the jackets, looking for fallen treasures.

"'Bet not, Tom.' I ran my hands over the row of thick woolen coats. Loose change clinked in some pockets; keys rattled in most every pocket. Pausing to jiggle one jacket, bouncing the keys, a spark ignited. It may not have lit the room or the coat on fire, but it definitely lit up an idea. 'Hey, Tom, get all the car keys out of everyone's pockets.'

"'From the jackets?' The words proceeded after lifting the first set, of course. 'Why?'

"'We're going to switch them all around!' Like kindling for fire, a metal pile built up on the floor. Snickers made their way around the edge of the door into the empty corridor. 'This is going to be great!'"

Tears of laughter rolled from Ariel's and Greg's eyes as he spoke.

"I can't imagine the scene in the parking lot!" Ariel said, laughing. "That's just terrible! And back then there were no clickers for the cars." She was doubled over from the images in her mind when her phone started vibrating. "Oh, shoot . . . I need to get this. Is that okay?"

"Sure, just ignore me," Greg said.

"I'm not ignoring you, it's for work. I'll make it quick."

"Hey, Stuart, what's going on?" She paused and got up from the table to step away from Greg. "Oh, I met him while he was visiting his partner in Seattle. . . . Yeah. Part of some hematology research but seems open to options."

Greg stopped chewing.

"That's right. We're meeting him next week." She paused. "Obscure leukemias. But I don't know exactly . . . I mean, I'm not a medical doctor or anything."

Greg choked.

Ariel looked towards the table. "Are you okay?" she whispered to him. "Hey, let me call you back in a bit, okay?" She hung up and returned to the table.

"What kind of consulting have you been working on?" Greg's eyes were almost menacing.

"I told you, I'm acting like an assistant for a client."

Greg's eyes were more serious than she'd ever seen them, no longer joking. "What kind of project?"

"A science project."

"Biotech? Right? One of the people you are after is an oncologist. A hematologist?"

"Yes," she said, picking up her fork. "The salad is really good; you should try it."

He wouldn't let her change the subject. "That's what I studied."

"I know."

"I was a research scientist."

"I know... I told you why we met. You kept thinking it was a joke."

"How'd we meet again? Why'd we meet?" he questioned her.

"A random chance on the Internet? It wasn't supposed to happen that way. I told you, my friend Stuart and I were just having fun thinking of the ways we could contact you. We had no idea you were on there or that you would email me." This time her voice cracked.

"A random meeting almost three thousand miles away? Bullshit. Did you want to find me? Did you try to meet me?" he asked, not hearing anything she was saying.

She didn't have time to say anything else; the rope snapped.

"Holy fuck." His eyes were wide. "It all comes together. Innocent little miss Ariel uses the Internet to hunt down the mark."

"You aren't a mark," she said. "A mark is someone who's going to be killed. Haven't you ever watched the movies?"

"Well, what do you want to know?" he asked, as if at an interrogation table.

"Nothing," she told him.

"Am I still on the list?"

"No."

"Ha! There was a list! And I was on it!" The inventiveness of his mind, fueled by spy movies, finally calmed down back at the house. Ariel curled up on the leather chair as the shadows from the hanging fan skipped along the floor.

Greg reclined on the sofa and muted the TV with the press of a button after Brandon went to bed. "It's been an interesting few days. Actually, an interesting year. First, you tell me you're skeptical about my investments and now this. I think it is you I shouldn't be trusting. Don't come out here anymore."

"Okay. I won't, and I understand."

"Oh, it is simple as that, 'okay, I won't — obviously you don't care about anything."

"What are you talking about, Greg. You just asked me not to come visit you anymore, and I said ok. I am not going to make a fuss about it."

"So our friendship means nothing? You've really been playing me this whole time?"

"That is not what I said at all. Respectfully, I am listening to what you just asked of me - not to come out. It has nothing to do with playing you or what value I placed on a friendship. But because this is the last time I will see you - unless something changes - what I said about Gabe is true, and hopefully you haven't sent him more money. He is not a good man. He is a criminal and if anyone is using you, it is him. I am asking you to be careful - not for me - but for yourself. Be careful, Greg."

"Of course I've sent him more money. We are in the middle of a project. Do you think I am stupid? Do you think I didn't do my diligence? But what do I know, I am only a doctor, right?"

"Okay, Do what you think is best."

"Whatever."

Ariel waited a moment before saying, "Thanks for letting us stay tonight. We won't wake you when we leave in the morning."

"Don't worry about it," he said congenially. "Just don't stomp down the stairs or anything, plus my door will be shut, so I won't hear you. And I'm locking it," he added.

Ariel didn't say anything.

"Don't you want to know why I said that?"

Ariel stood and draped the throw over the back of the chair before leaving the room. "I imagine that you are locking it to feel more secure. Maybe you are trying to make me feel I am not trust worthy. That is your opinion, not mine." He got up, following her to the stairwell, where his touch froze her. Turning cautiously, she faced him, preparing for whatever was coming next.

"I thought you were the one," he told her like she had ruined his life.

"What?" Ariel said, taken aback, not expecting to feel his lips upon hers for the first time. "What are you doing now?" She pushed him away.

"Kissing you," he gently whispered.

Ariel sighed, shaking her head, "No. Greg." then turned and went up to her room.

Early the next morning, she quietly slipped from the house.

***

The thought of Gabe Acero was now on the forefront of her mind when she returned home. She'd warned Greg, that was good, but Gabe good. The glow of Ariel's laptop screen cast sharp shadows across her dimly lit apartment. She sat hunched over her desk, eyes scanning line after line of account numbers, offshore transfers, shell company registrations. Gabe was careful—but not careful enough.

She tucked her phone between her shoulder and ear as she typed. The call had already rung twice.

Pick up.

Finally, a click. A familiar voice came through the line, low and alert. "Didn't expect to hear from you."

"I need a favor," Ariel said, still typing. "How hard is it to flag a dual passport holder moving money between the U.S. and the Dominican Republic?"

A pause. "Depends. What are we talking about here?"

"Two passports—American and Dominican. Offshore accounts. Investments tied up in real estate. More than a few questionable partners." She glanced at a file on her desk, flipping through transaction records. "And he's bleeding a few American citizens dry."

"Legally or otherwise?"

Ariel exhaled sharply. "Financial manipulation. Coercion. And if I had to guess? Probably threats, too."

The voice on the other end sighed. "You always bring me the fun ones. Name?"

"Gabriel Acero." Ariel paused, gripping her pen. "State Department already has whispers about him, but no one's pulling the trigger. He's got connections, but he's not untouchable. If someone—hypothetically—filed a request to flag his movements, what would it take to get eyes on him?"

A chuckle. "Ariel, you know how this works. I can look into it, but unless there's a clear national security risk, we're talking bureaucracy, slow-moving wheels. If he's just a con artist—"

"He's not just a con artist." Ariel's voice dropped, sharp

and certain. "I've spoken to him, there is a lot more going on under the surface of just moving American-earned money into accounts we can't track. And he's isolating Greg from anyone who questions it."

Silence. Then—"You think he's got Greg under control?"

"I know he does." She rubbed her temple, thinking of the last time she spoken with Greg. Defensive. Irritated. He didn't want to hear it. He never wanted to hear it.

"You don't know what you're talking about, Ariel."

But I do, Greg. I really do.

The voice on the other end exhaled. "Alright. Send me what you have. I'll see if we can get his name flagged at entry points. No promises, but if he's sloppy, something will stick."

"Appreciate it," Ariel said, closing her laptop.

"You sure you don't want to warn Greg outright?"

Ariel let out a dry laugh. "I have. He doesn't listen." She stood, stretching. "But eventually? He'll wish he had."

She ended the call, turning back to her desk.

She rubbed her chin recalling the wire Greg had made in front of her, one million two-hundred thousand dollars.

Oh, what a tangled web we weave, when first we practice

to deceive. The words echoed in Ariel's mind as she stared at the ceiling, the dim light from the laptop casting long shadows across the room. She wasn't sure who the warning was really for—Gabe, Greg thought he was the one weaving. He thought he was playing the game. But Gabe had seen him coming from a mile away, had known exactly what kind of man he was dealing with.

Greg, with his brilliant mind, his grand ideas, his absolute certainty that he was always the smartest person in the room. A man who believed rules were meant to be bent, if not broken outright—as long as he was the one doing the bending. And now, faced with a man like Gabe, he had convinced himself that he was still in control.

Ariel had seen this kind of arrogance before. It never ended well.

Greg. What have you gotten yourself into?

Chapter Nineteen

It's a fool's heart that misses the signs. Signs Ariel would never forget. Signs that were then branded on her soul, eternally.

"After several weeks of reflecting on her situation with Greg, Ariel was in the midst of planning her first trip to South America for her own private chocolate quest when Greg called," I said.

"Why did he keep talking with her?" Damion asked drearily.

"Well, they'd been in contact because they were sort of already working together trying to get funding for his company. So, although they weren't planning on re-establishing a friendship, both of them were people who followed through, come rain or shine. She'd kept most of their conversations focused, business oriented. But then after the funding fell through and ENSA was no more, he kept calling. And eventually, she began to open up. He was excited to hear about her upcoming adventure and invited her to stop on the way out of the country."

"So, their friendship resumed?" Damion asked.

"Yes, it resumed. He called her daily and made plans for her to go to Florida before heading further south into the cacao belt that follows the equator."

* * *

They hadn't seen much of Stuart since his marriage. But, Ariel got calls periodically regarding work, and that was about all. Then life shifted as it does sometimes—unexpectedly. The next call came from Stuart's wife.

"Ariel?" Her voice was young, and soft, and sounded on the verge of cracking.

"Misty?" Ariel asked, making sure it was who she thought it was. "Is everything okay?"

"Ariel?" This time Misty's voice did crack. "Oh, Ariel. Stuart . . ." That was about all she got out.

"Take your time, sweetheart. Stuart what?" Ariel tried calming her.

"Oh, Ariel, Stuart died." Misty began crying. "He died."

With her heart in check, Ariel asked Misty if she needed anything or if there was anything she could do.

"No, it all happened so suddenly. He took a medication, an antibiotic. He had an allergic reaction, and—" Misty's voice softened to barely a whisper. "It was over."

Ariel and the boys attended the services, which were more a celebration of Stuart's life than a formal farewell. The gathering spilled across Stuart and Misty's backyard. Ariel sat quietly, her gaze steady, taking in the ebb and flow of emotions around her. The boys sat beside her, their expressions a mix of thoughtfulness and sorrow.

Gresham broke the silence. "How long should we stay? He was part of our life so differently than everything here. I think I want to go home and remember him there. Would that be okay?" He looked at Ariel with the kind of directness he had always possessed, even as a child.

David nodded slightly, his face pale, his voice low. "I agree. I think we should go home. I'm not feeling very well."

Ariel studied them for a moment. She understood. This space, though filled with love and remembrance, wasn't theirs—it didn't hold the memories they shared with Stuart, the moments that had mattered most to them. "Of course," she said, her voice warm and steady. "Let's find Misty first."

They rose together, making their way through the clusters of mourners to find her. Ariel embraced her when they found her. "I'm so sorry," she said softly. The boys followed suit.

"I'm sorry, boys," Misty said. "He was so proud of you."

Once their goodbyes were said, they made their way home. The drive was quiet. Each of them was lost in their own thoughts, processing the day in their own way. By the time they reached the house, dusk had begun to settle, painting the world in soft, muted colors.

In the days and weeks that followed, the energy within their home shifted, subtly but unmistakably. The air carried an echo of Stuart's absence, a quiet reminder of the space he had once filled. She had never allowed herself to imagine what life would feel like if he weren't out there somewhere. Even in the years when their lives had diverged and his focus had shifted to his marriage, she had taken comfort in the knowledge of his presence. It had been enough.

Now, without him, there was a stillness she couldn't quite name. But even in the midst of their grief, smiles began to find their way into the rooms again. The boys would share a memory, and laughter would follow, unbidden but welcome.

Ariel often sat in the quiet hours, reflecting on all that had been and all that remained. She didn't know what life without Stuart fully meant yet, but she did know this: grief and joy could live side by side, and even in absence, love didn't disappear.

David looked contemplative as he and Ariel sat by the cottonwood-lined bank of the Yakima River in Eastern

Washington. Summer in July was just heading into full swing. Hikes, bonfires, treasure hunts, and plans for the fall filled the bright sunny days.

"You know something interesting?" she asked.

"What's that?"

"You and Stuart. I have gotten to share over half my life with you both. You have been in my life longer than you haven't been. Stuart was there for twenty-three years and you for twenty-two and counting." She smiled. "I am so thankful. I am so thankful we got to share our lives together. I love you so much, Davie."

David put his arm around her shoulders momentarily, "I don't know if I want you and Brandon going into South and Central America alone. You really need to be careful traveling."

"We will. I have security in each location and the guides are checked out. It'll be okay."

The river murmured softly, its current catching the glint of the setting sun. David stood moving to the water's edge, a skipping stone turning over in his hand. Ariel watched him, noting the way his shoulders tensed, his gaze fixed but distant. A shadow lingered behind his eyes, deeper than fatigue, sharper than the passage of time.

"How are you doing? Are you okay?" she asked, her voice low and tender.

His fingers tightened around the stone for a moment before he answered. "Yeah, I'm fine. Just have a lot on my mind recently, that's all. And I want you to be safe," he added.

Ariel moved closer, offering him a smooth stone from the ground. "Is there something you want to talk about, sweetheart?"

David turned the stone over in his palm, his jaw tightening. "Yes, and no," he said, his eyes flickering to the river as though searching for words in its endless flow. "I just... can't put my feelings into words."

He drew back his arm and skipped the stone across the water. It skimmed the surface three times before sinking, leaving faint ripples in its wake. "Something is changing," he said finally, his voice steady but low. "With Stuart dying, and two of my friends dying in Afghanistan. It's big. And it's... hollow."

Ariel tilted her head, her brows knitting. She stayed quiet, sensing the weight of what he wasn't saying.

David exhaled, his breath heavier than the moment called for. "I am feeling a bit lost, Mom. I can't watch the news because all I see is gaslighting. The government, the media, corporations—they're all working together. It's everywhere, this... this gaslighting. Every day, from every direction. The food industry, the health industry—even the ones that claim they're different, holistic, organic—it's all the same game. They want us unwell. They thrive on it. What kind of world does this?"

Ariel's lips parted, but she held back. She wanted him to keep going.

"Think about it," David pressed, his voice gaining an edge. "The worse we are—physically, emotionally, mentally — Every system, every structure, it's designed to keep us dependent. To keep us feeling like we're never good enough, never whole. It's like a spiderweb, and we're caught, struggling, feeding it."

He broke off, gripping another stone. The silent rush of the river their only audience.

"I don't know why I feel it so deeply," he murmured, the words quieter now, meant almost for himself. "But I know it's real. And it's getting worse."

David tossed the stone into the river, this time letting it sink without a skip. His hand trembled slightly as he turned back to Ariel.

Ariel's hand found his back, her touch light but steady.

He turned to her, his eyes glassy but unwavering. "I'm tired, Mom. Tired of how fake everything feels. I'm lonely. Everyone's glued to their screens, chasing things that don't matter. I just want someone who... Someone who'd rather watch the stars than a feed."

He handed her a smooth, amber-veined stone he'd been holding, its surface polished smooth by the river. She accepted it silently, her fingers brushing his as she took it.

They sat together on the riverbank for a long time, Ariel's arm holding his broad shoulders, the only sound the rhythmic rush of water over stone. He rested his head on her shoulder for a minute.

"Thanks for listening, Mom," he said at last, his voice softer now, the tension ebbing. He reached for another stone and handed it to her, a small grin tugging at his lips. "On another note, what do you think about culinary school?

She let out a light laugh. "Now, culinary school sounds pretty good."

"When I'm done with all this—school, the military—I'd like to give it a shot," he said.

Ariel nodded, looking out at the river as the rays of sunlight refracted below the surface. "I think you'd be wonderful at it... Do you want to come with Brandon and me? Take this semester off?"

"No, I'll be fine." Then he pondered the idea. "Well. I'll think about it."

"Okay." Ariel nodded. "Just remember you are more than welcome to come along."

Brandon ran over with handfuls of bread scraps.

"Quick, David, the ducklings!"

August arrived, and Gresham and David were headed back to their schools, their absence already felt in the quiet corners of the house. Ariel watched them prepare, their bags packed with precision, their goodbyes filled with promises to call. With the familiar ache of their leaving, her thoughts soon turned to the road ahead. She and Brandon were setting out to uncover chocolate mysteries. The purpose lingered in her mind like an unsolved riddle, drawing her forward.

Their first stop was Greg's house. It wasn't part of the official journey, but it felt essential. They went over plans, over maps spread across the kitchen table, marked with pencil lines tracing their route. Ariel hovered over them, fingers skimming the edges of well-worn paper. Brandon moved between research and small tasks, helping Greg tighten a loose hinge here, clear a space there. He even swept out the garage.

"Here," Greg said, handing her an envelope filled with emergency cash. "Be careful." His car sat idling under the shaded curbside check-in for Delta Airlines at the Sarasota airport.

"We'll be fine. You and I have gone over every scenario a hundred times," Ariel told him as he hugged her tightly. "And it's not like I've never traveled before."

He lifted their bags from the trunk. "Just don't go out alone. You'll be fine with Teresa [Greg's oncology partner who would also be in the area]. If you want, she said she'd join you when you leave the Dominican Republic for the other countries. She's heading to Colombia anyway to check on our oncology floor at the hospital there."

"Okay, I'll talk to her about it when we get there." They embraced in one more quick hug. "Thanks for the help, and your advice, and your concerns." Ariel and Brandon each swung a duffle bag to their shoulders. "I'll keep you abreast of the happenings ... or if anything interesting arises."

The trips between the Dominican Republic (where she would check on the Ocoa Bay winery which was one of the properties Greg had purchased with Gabe — who told Greg the purchase price for the raw land was seven million dollars when it was only three-hundred thousand), Venezuela, Colombia, and Guatemala created a magnificent backdrop to her final Ecuadorian destination, where over four thousand years prior, an awakening of sorts had occurred. Where long ago, in the ancient tropical lowlands, a spiritual alchemist bunkered in privacy. He sacrificed a handful of dried beans to the grinding stone. Herbs, fungi, and honeyed water were added to the paste. Coating his tongue, a spark of fire soared into the sky, marking time—an astrological reading.

The power of the beans moved secretively between mystics, reaching other tribes' nobilities. With advancing cultures, it added power to trading. It was said that when the Olmec of South-Central Mexico introduced their cocoa to the Mayans, others were already altering the plant, attempting to change its properties to increase production. Eventually, the original plant was found only in a long-forgotten legend.

It was this enigmatic myth that stirred within Ariel and had been stirring for much longer than the recent few hours she'd spent in her loose saddle, which rolled with the meandering sway of her horse. The myth swelled in the back recesses of her heart.

I should've brought us something to eat, Ariel thought.

A breeze moved through, darkening the sky beneath the tall canopy.

I think I've been here. The lids of her eyes draped, searching through years of mentally stored documentaries. Her mind's films flickered with the horse's rhythm. When? How would I know this place? I wasn't here with Stuart when we looked for that cacao all those years ago. In her mind a vine sprouted . . . a mist coasted over a fallen log in the Oregon rainforest, and a yellow rain slicker draped over her hands; the night sky opened, and she knelt beneath the stars. Then the images moved to a pine tree next to an old shack, and she was on her knees beneath the midnight sky burying a jar.

The horse swayed enough to awaken her from the daydream.

I've got to tighten these straps or I'm going to fall off.

"Podemos detener por favor? Can we stop please?" Her Spanish was just as shaky as the saddle as she called to their guide, Pedro.

"Yes. We stop," he said. Although heavily accented, his English was good.

Reins looped a branch where a few yellow fruits lay beside her feet.

"Hey, Mom, look at that!" Brandon said, reaching down to get it. "It looks like a little cocoa pod." As he reached for it, a blade sliced through the air, cutting deep into the twisted wooden trunk.

"What are you doing?" Ariel shrieked while Brandon quickly retracted his arm.

"This plant es prohibida," the guide told her.

Several more small pods rolled to her feet, barely bigger than the palm of her hand. Deep mulberry-colored veins ran in lacy patterns at the base of their stems.

"A prohibited plant? Why?" She cracked one of the pods against a sharp rock; the ivory-covered beans were lovely. "They look like cacao," she said curiously, showing it to Brandon. He nodded his head.

"Mira. See?" The tip of the guide's knife pointed at the vein before tossing it away. "This might make you very sick."

"So, it'll kill you?" Brandon asked.

Pedro shook his head in answer. "It was given from the gods to the spiritualist leaders thousands of years ago," he explained. "Advising only they consume it. It is a very rare legend to find this plant. When the Spanish came this planta was hidden and then cut to be safe from trade. Legend says it was removed to hide the connection to the — how I say... ahh... supernatural. I don't know how this one grew."

A coatimundi slinked from its hiding place, took in the surroundings, and retreated after grabbing the open pod.

The blade lifted once more to attack the root.

"Pedro, wait!" Ariel touched his arm. "Please, no, please don't kill it, not yet. Please wait until we come back down."

Reluctantly Pedro sheathed his blade.

"I want to take the pods home with me, maybe the root if possible." She thought for a second. "If I tasted one, would it kill me?"

"I don't think it will kill you," he said. "It is only legend. I not see it before. But if it is the plant, it will not kill you."

"I think I want to try it. I know this isn't the best place, but there's something..."

Ariel closed her eyes and placed the pulp-covered bean on her tongue. Sweetness melted away, leaving the brittle core behind. She swallowed, the taste lingering like a whisper of antiquity.

She swung onto the horse, energy quivering inside her—like a monarch breaking free, like a buried envelope rising, its vine unfurling toward the sky. A name bloomed upon its ivy.

David?

She saw him—his thoughtful, deep brown eyes—as he leaned in, breathing in the scent of delicate flowers. Petals brushed the satin of his skin. Then his image wavered, slipping away.

Wait, Davie. Please wait.

And then, the dream returned, as it had so many times before. They crouched together, hidden in the woods, hands digging into the earth. Beans spilled into his cupped palms, his fingers cradling them sacredly.

Behind them, the world burned. But in the clearing beyond the thicket, light streamed from the heavens. Seven ethereal figures emerged, their presence humming with something beyond time. One extended a hand for David.

He turned to leave.

"Wait, David! Wait." A panic rose in her voice. *"Where are you going? Stay here. Please."*

"It's time for me to go home. I'll always love you." His words faded with the encasing mist.

Ariel and Brandon spotted two more of the strange cacao on their afternoon jaunt. The plants were near one another and Ariel convinced Pedro, who owned a plant nursery for cacao, not to kill them. "Please, I will pay you money to protect these. Will you do that for me?" she asked.

"How much?" he asked, interested.

"I will pay you for one year, or until we figure out what to do with them, and I will send you money every month. Would you be willing to do that?" Ariel asked, hoping to make a deal that benefited both of them.

"Yes, I will keep them safe for you." He nodded in agreement.

"Oh, thank you, Pedro. And please keep this private; don't tell anyone these are here. Okay?" she asked, with a sneaky suspicion that she'd found the elusive cacao.

"Okay," he said, shaking her hand. "They are safe."

"You are their protector. Thank you."

When Ariel and Brandon returned to their hotel room, she took the pods they'd found and prepped them for shipping—or smuggling.

"Mom, did you feel anything when you ate that bean today?" His words were laced with inquiry. "'Cause I ate one too. And I felt, well, I tasted—more of a suspicion of something. Do you think it was poison? Are we going to be, okay?"

"I felt that almost-something too . . . I don't think we are going to die. I don't think it is poisonous." She looked at him. "But, you know what I do think?"

He shook his head.

"I think what we found was the last remnant of the original cacao. If that is what we found, you and I have just touched an incredibly special history."

After all their fairy tale cocoa years, they were sharing a secret that had been calling to them the whole way.

Brandon grabbed Ariel's cell phone. "Guys, you won't believe it!" he exclaimed when both David and Gresham were on the line. "You won't believe it. We found the cacao. We found it, and we ate a bean." Brandon went on to tell his brothers all about their trip and the cacao. "We are bringing pods back so you can try some too!"

On the way to the airport, Ariel called Greg, who answered on the first ring. "Hey, how's it going down there?"

"I think we may have found something pretty interesting.

Brandon and I could stop by on the way home and show you, if you'd like? We are staying on for a few more weeks, Pedro is helping us with some of the beans."

"Just let me know and I'll pick you up at the airport. See you soon."

"How in the world did you get these through customs?" Greg laughed, closing the door behind them. The box landed softly on the kitchen counter, in a square sunlit patch next to the sink.

Her answer was a sideways glance with a sly smile.

The blade moved gently between the taped flaps. Somewhere near the beach, Brandon's laughter echoed faintly, lacrosse, salt air, sunlight, playing inside the quiet of Ariel's heart.

"I'll just be outside, talking to Tom," Greg said after a pause, reading her silence the way someone reads wind on water. "Let me know if you need anything."

She nodded without turning. The door clicked closed behind him.

The pods inside the box were smaller than they looked in the jungle, but they still carried the shimmer of an unspoken history. She laid them on the counter one by one. Their skins were mottled, sun-darkened, each patterned like pressed bark. Beneath them, caught beneath the last fold of the box, an envelope blinked up at her, rough paper, stitched at the corners. The beans.

She unfolded the packet.

They had dried well. She could still see the small nick in one of them, the place where Pedro's thumbnail had cracked the husk before packing them away. These were the ones they'd fermented and dried separately—quietly, outside the scope of the official samples. The ones he'd called para ti, no más.

She roasted them low. The aroma slipped into the corners of the house—not sweet, not too bitter, but deep. It moved through the walls without permission, without warning. A different kind of time gathered in the room.

She ground the beans with a slow rhythm, adding a few drops of warm water until the paste darkened to the color of rain-polished soil. Her fingers rolled the paste into itself, again and again. No distractions. No clocks. Just the steady weight of something she had never understood but had never forgotten.

One of the beans had broken during roasting. Its edge was jagged, glistening faintly.

She lifted the nibs. Held them between her fingers.

Small. Misshapen. Perfect.

She bit them.

And everything fell away.

She sank to her knees.

Not gently. Not with drama. Just—down. The tile met her. The ceiling vanished. She wasn't in the kitchen anymore.

She was eleven.

There was soil under her nails. A jar in her hand. The old pine leaned over her like a witness. The envelope pressed flat beneath the Mason jar's lid. Her knees cold, her hands shaking.

The taste spread, slow and low. Not sweetness—no, never that. This was older. This was stone, and bark, and the scent of wet moss after the stars had gone.

Only the presence of a feeling so pure it was nameless— a feeling woven within her she had carried all this time. A secret buried with the beans and had somehow made its way back through her mouth, into her bones.

The flavor blossomed delicately.

Opening.

And opening.

Time unspooled around her. She was three. She was thirty. She was ageless. She was part of the landscape that ran beneath rivers and seedbeds, and carried by wind. The pod had waited. The beans had not spoiled. They had not vanished.

They had waited.

The kitchen was silent as she moved beyond the world of Ought, touching the connect to the Land Ought Not, where life is whole.

When she finally rose from the floor, the paste lingered on her tongue; her hands moved differently and her mind expanded. There was no rush, no overwhelming surge—only a deepening awareness. She became acutely conscious of the space around her: the texture of the air, the faint hum of life in the room, the pulse of her own heartbeat, steady and strong. The plants near the window seemed cognizant, their presence vivid, each leaf evidence of something she couldn't name but knew she was part of. The sun filtering through the glass turned the air golden, and she let herself breathe, breathe in something that reached beyond the physical.

She turned her gaze inward, testing the boundaries of this newfound clarity, and found there were none. Her thoughts stretched into the quiet hum of existence, touching truths that now made themselves known. She didn't question it. There was no need. This was a language that always had been, one hidden well below the surface of modern life.

The cocoa's presence didn't fade, but it settled itself into her body and mind as though it had always belonged.

She stayed still for a moment longer before zipping from

the kitchen, spoon in hand, and her socked feet skidded before practically taking flight through the door.

"Oomph." She ran into Greg, nearly missing Brandon, who had just returned from his game. "Ariel, be careful."

"Taste this," she said excitedly. "No wonder the medicine men said this cocoa was poisonous, I bet they said that to protect it. I think we found it, Brandon. I think we really found it."

"No thanks," Greg said, stepping back with a smirk. "I'll stick to real chocolate—this is a mess only you'd love." Her excitement faltered, but she forced a smile—disappointed, in herself. He turned away.

"Not just her," Brandon said taking the spoon. "We've been trying to find this for a long time, right mom? The story of cacao, is real! I knew it! I knew it right when we tasted it earlier." He practically skipped to the kitchen.

Ariel nodded. "It's on the kitchen counter. You don't need much at all. I had maybe a half-teaspoon."

Greg watched Brandon head into the kitchen. "What does he mean?" He asked. "What's the story of the chocolate?"

"Years ago, like twenty-three years ago, I was on a project with my partner Stuart to find a mysterious cacao. This guy who hired us said he'd tasted some incredible chocolate given to him by his secretary, and that was twenty years before he came to us

A Simple Twist of Chocolate

to try and hunt it down. He'd been obsessed with it ever since, searching for it off and on that whole time," Ariel explained. "He struggled to put the effects into words, just that he'd never felt so clear and alive and connected before or after. Stuart and I searched for months in multiple countries and came to the conclusion that he was smitten with his young secretary, drunk on drink and on passion, and his memory of the experience was a combination of all that. Well, that and amazing-tasting chocolate."

"But you didn't find this?" Greg asked, pointing to the little pods.

Ariel shook her head. "Nope, we found a small plantation in Venezuela that produced one of the most incredible cocoas I've ever experienced. That was what we brought back to him. But it wasn't this." She held one of the small pods. "Then, before you and I met, a few thoughts, memories really, made me think there was something else to the cacao this man was after. I had tasted something when I was young. Something I wasn't supposed to find in my father's files. I remember thinking that if this man had such an impression made upon him, there had to be something more to it than a box of Valentine's Day candy. And that's when the boys and I learned how to make chocolate. Brandon was beside me while researching fabled stories, their history, and modern-day uses and health benefits. We even developed some that reversed tooth decay and thought of selling it to orthodontists and dentists, hot chocolates for school fundraisers, and many other things, including a cocoa skincare line, even plans for a cocoa hotel, cocoa spa, and cocoa cafe. Daydreams really, but there was always something missing. Something I could never quite put my finger on."

"This cacao... is this what you and Stuart found that man?" Greg asked again.

"No, like I said, we found a type of Criollo beans back then—the Porcelana Criollo. I gave you some when we first met." Greg nodded in recollection. "You remember the amazing flavor? I mean unbelievable flavor. That's what we thought he'd tasted. And it seemed to satisfy his quest. None of us knew about what's in the kitchen now or that something like that even existed," Ariel continued. "But it stuck with me, the food of the gods."

***

Ariel's phone buzzed.

Seeing the caller, she walked away from Greg for privacy.

"Hey Karoline, Did you find anything?"

"Your guy? Gabe. He's washing money. And not for the usual white-collar crooks."

She sat up straighter. "That's what I thought. He was really interested in the port building in Santo Domingo."

"Well, you were right about the cartel — and it is worse." Papers shuffled in the background. "He's moving cash - hitting accounts linked to high-seas smuggling ops. Know what that means?"

Ariel's stomach tightened. Ariel rubbed her collarbone. Modern sea piracy. Armed groups operating in the shadows, hijacking cargo ships, smuggling weapons, moving drugs across borders where no one was watching. Ruthless, unpredictable. And Gabe? He was helping bankroll them.

She glanced at the screen again. One of the flagged accounts was linked to a company posing as an import-export firm. Another was tied to a Dominican shipping conglomerate.

"This isn't just fraud and small potatoes international wire fraud anymore," she muttered. "This is flat out international crime."

"And the Feds will care a hell of a lot more about that than some guy fleecing a few high rolling doctors."

Her mind raced. If Greg was tied to any of these accounts, even unknowingly, he could be dragged under with Gabe when this all came crashing down.

She needed to get him out.

Before it was too late.

Ariel dialed another number—one she didn't call unless it

was serious.

A clipped, professional voice answered. "This is Keller."

"I need an urgent review of a U.S. citizen's financial ties to offshore laundering operations."

"Who are we looking at?"

"Gabriel Acero."

A long pause. Then—"Send me everything you have. And Ariel?"

"Yeah?"

"If this guy is mixed up with both the cartel and modern pirates, you need to watch your back."

Chapter Twenty

"Did you know, no matter the kind of cocoa you use to craft a piece of chocolate—whether dark or milk — only a single drop of water is enough to bind melted chocolate into something entirely different? It doesn't take much, just that one drop, to change its nature. You may not see the effects at first, even if you care for it tenderly. The transformation happens quietly, subtly, and by the time you notice, it's already too late to undo what's been done.

"When I was a child, dreams of what the future looked like were distant, like heat vapor rising from the hot cement a mile before me. The flowers grew in the spring, even when the ashes from Mount St. Helens blanketed them. There were birds chirping and butterflies floating, contrasted by the periodic black shadows of ghouls and gloved clouds stealing the moon... But nothing can prepare you for nuclear devastation."

***

2014

When Ariel and Brandon returned from their trip, her thoughts immediately turned to Thanksgiving break. On one of their usual Skype calls, she and her boys were all excited and making plans for what they would like to do on their holiday.

"I can hardly wait to see you guys," Ariel said. "I got your tickets today and sent them to your emails."

"Thanks, Mom. I can hardly wait to be home and go for a night hike to watch the stars, just like the old days," Gresham said. "But, until then, I need to get going to class. See you, guys. I love you."

"Love you too, Gresham," they all chimed together, watching his screen blink out.

"Love you, David," Brandon said, scooting by Ariel. "See you."

"See you, Brandon. Love you."

Ariel and David remained on the call. "Are you okay, Davie?" she asked gently, tilting her head. "You look a little warn. Is there anything I can do to help?"

"Yeah. I'll be okay," he replied.

Ariel noticed. "Would you like to come home sooner? I can change your ticket easily. I'd love to have you here, to help with our move."

David paused. "Maybe," he said, his voice low.

Ariel a ripple of unease rained through her. Her lungs filled and sent him her most reassuring smile before saying goodbye.

Days passed. She found herself glancing at her phone more often than usual, even though they spoke daily. There was a flicker of unease growing into a steady hum. Then, a text from David came through: What is life aside from a random grouping of molecules developing for no real point or reason? The words felt like a weight dropping into her lap. Her chest tightened as she read on, her hands trembling slightly.

She immediately called him. The call went unanswered. Her fingers tapped out a message quickly, but her heart was pounding: Davie, please call me.

Finally, her phone rang. Ariel's heart didn't know whether to slow down or speed up as she answered. "Please listen to me, Davie," she said, heart heart clenching, holding itself together.

The line went silent for a moment.

"Are you there?" she pressed.

"I'm here," David replied, his voice barely above a whisper.

"Maybe it would be a good idea for you to talk with someone," she suggested gently, even as her mind churned, her instincts screaming at her to do more.

"Maybe we can talk with someone together? Can you help me?" David's voice cracked slightly, and Ariel felt the weight of his pain settle heavily on her own chest.

"Of course, Davie. We'll do that right now."

The session they managed to schedule was weeks away, and Ariel found herself caught in a storm of helplessness and determination. Even though they all spoke daily, she questioned if it was enough. Brandon's daily 3:33 call to David had become a ritual Ariel quietly cherished—less a whimsy now, and more a thread that held the edges of their days together.

Three days later, her phone buzzed again. The message moved her breath to her throat: Mom, I love you. I will always remember my childhood and the feeling of home when I was by your side . . .

The words blurred as tears filled her eyes. Without hesitation, she dialed. When David answered, her voice was steady, though her hands trembled. "David, are you thinking of doing something? Are you thinking of ending your life?"

"Yes," he admitted quietly, "but I'm afraid I don't know how."

She reached deep into the well of love she had for him. "I need you to go to the hospital, okay?" she said firmly, her voice softening.

Silence.

"Davie . . . do you remember when you were little? You'd sit behind me in the car, and I'd reach back and hold your hand while I drove?"

He didn't respond right away. "Yeah . . ." His voice was thick with tears.

"I'm reaching back there now. Take my hand, Davie," Ariel said, her own tears slipping silently down her face.

There was a long pause. Then, quietly, he replied, "Okay. I'll go.

Greg who was visiting her while house hunting, saw panic setting in over Ariel's face as she walked inside, "Ariel?"

"Greg, I need a favor. It's David. He agreed to go to the hospital, but I don't want him sitting in the waiting room for hours. Can you call ahead? Talk to the attending, physician to physician?"

"Why is he going to the hospital?"

Ariel's throat tightened, "He sent me a text, Greg. He... he's in a bad place. He needs help now."

"I'll call the ER and push for a hold."

An hour later David sent a text - They sent me home—Ariel felt the ground shift beneath her feet.

She called immediately. "How are you feeling?" she asked, her voice trembling with the effort to remain calm.

"They said I'm fine, Mom," David replied, but his words didn't carry the reassurance she desperately needed.

Ariel whispered urgently to Greg, "They sent him home." Panic simmered beneath her composed tone.

"David, do you want me to come up there? I can get the first flight in the morning."

"No, I mean, if you want to, but I am going to be in school and at work, so you'll just be sitting in the hotel."

"I don't mind. I want to see you." Ariel tried to keep her voice calm, not allowing her panic to take over.

"Mom, I think I just needed to talk to someone. They said I was okay. I will see you in a few weeks, anyway."

Going back into the office Ariel found Greg.

"They sent him home. Can you call the doctor and see what happened? Please?"

"I did. He said David's a 'bright young man' and 'just in a rough patch.' They don't think he's a risk at all."

Ariel whispered, chills cascading down her arms. "They sent him home? Greg, you have to get him admitted."

Greg's voice rose slightly with irritation, "The doctor brushed it off—'He'll be fine over the weekend. Have him call Monday.' Monday, Ariel!"

Ariel left the room unsure what to do, returning moments later to sit across from Greg at the kitchen table, her hands wrapped tightly around a mug of untouched coffee. The lines around her eyes were deeper, carved by worry. Greg leaned back, his arms crossed, watching her with a doctor's practiced calm.

"I need to go," she said, her voice trembling as she finally broke the silence. "David needs me."

Greg tilted his head, his expression unreadable, clinical even. "Ariel, let's take a step back. I get that you're worried. But let's be honest—what are you actually going to accomplish by going there?"

She flinched. "I don't know. Just... being there? Letting him know he's not alone."

"And then what?" Greg leaned forward; his voice quiet but firm. "You show up, and it's awkward. He's probably embarrassed. You can't fix this for him, Ariel. I won't let him slip through the cracks. Do you understand?"

The question hit the softest, oldest part of her.

Her childhood ghosts stirred immediately— pouring venom into her shredding heart. Foaming.

You make things worse.

You'll just hurt him even more, stupid Ariel.

She blinked at him, uncertainty pooling in her eyes. "But what if he needs—"

Her voice fought back inside her. *Don't make a mistake, Ariel. Trust your instincts.*

Then came the echoes returned, sharp and mocking. *Your instincts? Why would you even consider trusting yourself? What will it be? You're going to gamble with your son's life? Good. Luck.*

Every fiber of her being opened.

"I need to go."

Greg cut her off gently but firmly. "Ariel. Trust me on this. There's nothing you can do right now that will change anything."

His tone was steady, authoritative, the way she imagined he might speak to a patient or their family in the hospital. It was the voice of reason she'd sought, and yet... something in it twisted in her chest.

"I don't know what to do. I don't want to make a mistake." she whispered, her hands tightening around the mug.

"Exactly," he said. "That's why you need to let this play out. Give him space. If you crowd him, he'll shut down. Trust me. I've seen it a hundred times."

He's a doctor. She reminded herself, Trust him. He knows what he is talking about. I am panicking. Maybe I am not thinking clearly. Oh please, oh please help please. Help my David! She prayed.

She nodded slowly, swallowing the lump in her throat. "You're sure? I am asking you because I don't know what to do. I am desperate and want to make sure I am doing the right thing."

"I'm sure," he said.

Greg leaned back again, his hand resting on the table. His face softened, but not with reassurance—there was something else, a flicker of satisfaction that he quickly buried behind a professional mask. Ariel didn't notice.

She exhaled shakily, the decision settling into her bones with a hollow thud. "Okay. I won't go." Going against every fiber of her being.

"You're doing the right thing," Greg said, his voice kind now, a shade warmer than before. "David's lucky to have a mom who cares this much."

But as Ariel stared down at her untouched drink, a small, nagging voice in the back of her mind whispered that she'd left something undone. Something essential. Ariel closed her eyes, praying she had not just silenced the one voice she needed most—her own.

***

When Gresham had first left for school, Ariel found herself in the midst of transitions, both big and small. Among them was the difficult task of packing away the life they had built at the river house. Brandon's father had offered to store a few of her things in his garage. Among the items were three boxes she called "the mommy boxes." They were filled with fragments of her sons' childhoods—scrapbooks, handmade cards, little treasures she couldn't bear to part with. And in one of those boxes was something especially precious: her china doll, Kitty.

Kitty had been with Ariel through everything. As a child, the doll had absorbed every tear, every whispered secret, every ounce of love she had to give. An intimate piece of her wrapped in porcelain. But as the years passed and the river house filled with new memories, Kitty had been carefully packed away, waiting for the right moment to resurface.

Now, Ariel found herself drawn to that doll in a way she couldn't explain. It felt like Kitty was calling to her. The feeling was so strong that she picked up the phone and called Brandon's father.

"I was wondering if it would be okay if I got those boxes soon?" she asked, her voice light but insistent.

"Of course," he replied. "I'll be in the area in a few days. I can drop them by."

Relief flooded her. "Oh, thank you. Thank you so much."

When the boxes arrived the following week, Ariel placed them in the garage. She wanted to sort through them carefully, to take her time rediscovering the memories tucked inside. But the pull toward Kitty was too strong. A few days later, she opened the first box with quiet anticipation. She searched carefully. But when she finally came to where Kitty should have been, all she found was a small porcelain foot.

The air sent a sucker punch to her lungs. The doll—her doll—was gone. The pit in her stomach dropped so fast she had to grip the edge of the box to steady herself. A wave of nausea swept over her, and for a moment, she thought she might actually throw up.

Before another wave flushed through, she called Brandon's father.

"Hey, Ariel. What's up?" His voice was as cheerful as ever.

"Hi," she said, steadying herself. "It's nice to hear your voice." And it was true; he someone she trusted implicitly. "By any chance, have you seen my doll?" she asked, her voice carefully neutral.

"No," his voice cracked ever so slightly, "what doll?"

"It was in one of the boxes you dropped off."

"No, sorry, I haven't seen it," he said quickly. Too quickly.

The unease in her stomach twisted into something sharper, "Ok. Thank you." A half hour passed, but the nagging feeling wouldn't leave her alone. She called him again; her voice cracked this time.

"Hi again, are you sure you didn't see my porcelain doll?" she asked. "It's really important, and I know it was in that box."

Silence echoed through the cavernous space between them, the box observing their exchange. Then, at last, his voice spilled out from the dark, fragile and raw. "Oh, Ariel, I'm sorry. I'm so sorry. I don't know why I did it."

Sharp brambles of the woods she once wandered wrapped around her, constricting her heart, thick and unyielding. "Did what?"

"I threw it away," his voice splintering like a fallen branch underfoot.

"What?" The word left her lips, fragile as a single leaf carried by the wind.

"It was like... something came over me. I had to do it," he said. "I don't know why, Ariel. I'm so sorry. I did it just before I came over."

The phone slipped from her hand and landed with a muffled thud against the cement that had turned into the forest floor beneath her feet. Moss crept between her fingers as she knelt, her breaths shallow, each one pulling her further into the woods. Around her, the trees loomed impossibly tall, their bark etched with jagged scars. The air smelled of damp earth and rose with his voice filled with regret. "Ariel? Are you there?"

"I'm here," she whispered. "It's ok - Thank you for letting me know."

Fear and grief pressed against her, not like a wave but like the roots of the ancient oaks, wrapping tighter and tighter until her edges blurred, until she became part of the forest.

The knowing came then, deep and endless, pooling in her like a hollowed tree: what was lost would never be found again. Shaking but determined, she reached for her phone again. Her voice was calm, even steady, as she dialed David's number.

"Hi, sweetheart. How are things going up there?" Ariel asked, her voice as light as she could make it. She was sitting in her car, parked in the driveway, cradling the phone to her ear.

"It's okay," he replied, his voice calm but subdued. "A bit rainy and cold here, though. Are you going to be okay with your doctor's appointment tomorrow?"

"Yes, it's just a check-up; the doctors just want to see if I have an ulcer or something. It's an easy procedure, nothing to worry about," she assured him. "I love you, David. I want you to know how much you are loved."

There was a pause, a moment of quiet that felt heavier than usual. "I know, Mom," he said softly. "I love you too. And no matter what the future brings, hold your loved ones close."

"You're my loved one, Davie. Do you need anything?" she asked, trying to bridge the distance between them. "An umbrella, a warm coat?"

"No," David said. "I think I have everything I need. Thank you, though."

Ariel anxiety took hold of her hand as the call ended, but she convinced herself he sounded fine—tired, maybe, but fine, she told herself. She held onto his final words, repeating them in her mind like a mantra: I love you too.

What Ariel didn't know was that on his way home that afternoon, he took the bus to Walmart, where the hunting department displayed many arms in waiting, and upon leaving the store, he'd stopped to take one last photo of the beautiful autumn sunset.

That night, tears drenched his pillow as his life replayed in his mind. The words he wanted to say dripped into the padding, soaking it through, and the love he felt for his family drained into the warm safekeeping of time standing still.

In the morning, he cleaned his room, made his bed, turning the desperate weight filling his pillow over, hiding the large, painful tear stains. His cell phone and computer were placed on the cleared desk next to a box of bullets, with one removed.

His backpack carried a few items to the knoll above the backyard, where he sat upon the hill, allowing the early morning sun to grace his cheeks and the air to carry the harmonious birds' flight. All day he sat there in quiet meditation and reflection.

And when the sun was just beginning its descent, casting red against the autumn sky, storm clouds moved in. David stood alone, the rifle moved carefully into position.

A gentle breeze bowed the wheat over the rolling hills.

Tears began dripping from the hovering clouds, running with his own.

The shot cracked with the distant roll of thunder as his body fell to the earth.

* * *

Suicide is a thief that strikes without warning, stealing away moments you thought you'd have forever. The signs, if they existed at all, often reveal themselves too late. Ariel replayed those final conversations with David, holding her breath as if by some miracle time might rewind and she could pull him back.

But now, in hindsight, every word, every pause, every unspoken thing between them felt like a haunting trail of breadcrumbs she had failed to follow.

From a distance, while he was away at school, David's pain had been easier for him to hide. Ariel had known he was struggling—they had talked about it, faced those dark thoughts together. She had thought, she had hoped, that they'd crested those moments, that his heart had steadied into the rhythm of life again. She had let herself believe he was feeling better. She had convinced herself to believe he was okay.

But the truth, devastating in its clarity, shattered her. He had carried his pain so deeply, so quietly, that even love couldn't break through. It was a reality that suffocated her. The weight of his absence pressed down on her chest, making it impossible to breathe. And yet, somehow, she did. Somehow, Brandon and Gresham did. Somehow, they kept breathing, even in a world that no longer held their David.

Through this, she found a fragile thread of solace. Kitty, her china doll—the keeper of her childhood tears, her secrets, and her love—has been released. The pain of that loss had been a sharp, immediate thing, but now she imagined it differently. She imagined that the doll, filled with the spirit of her own love, had been released into the universe at just the right moment. That somehow, Kitty was there to meet David, so he wasn't alone.

A Simple Twist of Chocolate

This volume concludes here because my life required a silence that the narrative could not fill. It represents exactly as it occurred—sudden and absolute.

Thank you for walking through the first part of this journey with me.

Maren Muter

The story continues in Book Two.

The Chocolate Syndicate, Book II

The Chocolate Syndicate

A Simple Twist of Chocolate

www.ingramcontent.com/pod-product-compliance
Lightning Source LLC
LaVergne TN
LVHW041619060526
838200LV00040B/1349